TRADING 102

WILEY TRADING ADVANTAGE

TRADING 102

GETTING DOWN TO BUSINESS

SUNNY J. HARRIS

John Wiley & Sons, Inc.

NEW YORK • CHICHESTER • WEINHEIM • BRISBANE • SINGAPORE • TORONTO

This book is printed on acid-free paper. ∞

Copyright © 1998 by Sunny J. Harris. All rights reserved.
Published by John Wiley & Sons, Inc.

Published simultaneously in Canada.

This publication is designed to provide accurate and authoritative information in regard to the subject matter covered. It is sold with the understanding that the publisher is not engaged in rendering professional services. If professional advice or other expert assistance is required, the services of a competent professional person should be sought.

Designations used by companies to distinguish their products are often claimed by trademarks. In all instances where the author or publisher is aware of a claim, the product names appear in Initial Capital letters. Readers, however, should contact the appropriate companies for more complete information regarding trademarks and registration.

Material in this book is for educational purposes only. It should not be assumed that the methods, techniques, or indicators presented in this book will be profitable or that they will not result in losses. Past results are not necessarily indicative of future results. This is not a solicitation of any offer to buy or sell. Trading and investing are speculative and include risk of loss.

Hypothetical or simulated performance results have certain inherent limitations. Unlike an actual performance record, simulated results do not represent actual trading. Also, since the trades may not have been executed, the results may have under- or overcompensated for the impact, if any, of certain market factors, such as lack of liquidity. Simulated trading programs in general are also subject to the fact that they are designed with the benefit of hindsight. No representation is being made that any account will or is likely to achieve profits or losses similar to those shown.

Library of Congress Cataloging-in-Publication Data:
Harris, Sunny J.
    Trading 102: getting down to business / Sunny J. Harris.
      p. cm.—(Wiley trading advantage)
    Includes bibliographical references and index.
    ISBN 0-471-18133-1 (cloth : alk. paper)
    1. Portfolio management.   2. Portfolio management—Mathematics.
3. Stock-exchange.   4. Commodity exchanges.   I. Title.   II. Series.
    HG4529.5.H368   1998
    332.64—dc21   98-17659

Printed in the United States of America.

10 9 8 7 6 5 4 3 2 1

To my son Shelby Harris, whom I love endlessly, and to my father, now deceased, who was and still is my inspiration and my measuring stick; and most of all to Howard,* through Whom all things are possible.

And a special thanks to Jon Harris, who encouraged me to start trading in the 1970s, long before it was popular.

---

*From the children's prayer: "Our Father, Who are in Heaven, Howard be Thy name."

The human mind, once stretched to include a single new idea, does not shrink back to its original proportions.

■ Oliver Wendell Holmes

Until one is committed, there is hesitancy.

■ W. H. Murray

We must never assume that which is incapable of proof.

■ G. H. Lewes

Be sure of it; give me the ocular proof.

■ William Shakespeare

CONTENTS

Contents

PREFACE

Trading 101—How to Trade Like a Pro provided the essentials of how to get started in this seemingly difficult business. After the publication of *Trading 101—How to Trade Like a Pro,* readers called often saying "Why didn't you write this book sooner?" Furthermore, they wanted the next book completed so they could take the second step. Many, however, had already taken the second step on their own and fumbled; they had gone headlong into the danger zone without heeding the warnings and had lost their trading capital before beginning their homework. I hope this was not you.

There is so much more ground to cover in trading basics than could be put in one book, so *Trading 102—Getting Down to Business* takes your studies one step further.

The purpose of the first book was to introduce a perhaps heretofore scary concept to a wide audience and dissipate the element of fear. This second book uses the first as a prerequisite, builds on those concepts, refers to materials in the first book, and goes beyond it into the nuts and bolts of system design and running your trading business. It is meant to give you the necessary tools to put your plans in motion, whether you are trading for yourself or managing other people's money.

Just as there are many personality types in the general population, there are many different trading styles. As in the first book, again with the cooperation of Adrienne Laris Toghraie, this book includes a chapter on the emotional issues of trading. This chapter provides you with a self-assessment to help you make choices in your trading based upon your own personality.

Primarily this book addresses the science of trading. I will demonstrate how I design and test systems. I will show you logical and mathematical constructs that you may use in creating a sound system, or verifying that the system you are currently using is sound. Most importantly, you will learn quantitative measures of success. This book addresses the preparation one must make before even considering trading as a way of producing income.

Lastly, I will look at what it takes to put your plan into action and turn your trading into a real business. In this segment, I will begin with organization and time management, followed by a business plan for trading with tips on how to set up your own trading business. Every industry has its Personnel Department, its Human Resources, and its Industrial Counselors. Since traders are often loners, I include the do-it-yourself version of these important departments herein.

No matter how disciplined you are, if your system or methodology doesn't work, you will lose money. On the other hand, no matter how well your system works, if you don't follow it, you will again lose money. You must have both the science and the art of trading and be able to pull discipline and a good system together successfully.

For those of you who waited patiently, here it is. For those who jumped into the fray and incurred losses, you might use this book to break some bad habits and get back on track again. And for those who jumped in and are immensely successful, congratulations!

Note that throughout this book I will use the masculine pronouns generically, implying his/hers, he/she, him/her in all cases. Furthermore, all that I do, say, and provide is intended to be educational in nature and must not be misconstrued as trading advice.

—Sunny J. Harris
July, 1997

TRADING 102

1 PLAN YOUR WORK, THEN WORK YOUR PLAN

Regardless of how much preparation you make toward trading the markets, it's never enough. Furthermore, no matter how long you are in the business, you will continue to learn respect for the markets, and you will continue to learn new trading techniques. One is eternally a student of the markets.

Trading is a business fraught with peril. The market is governed by fear and greed: fear when the market has made a large move down and folks are afraid of losing more, and greed when the market is making new highs and everyone wants some of the perceived profits. There are bulls and there are bears—and then there are just plain chickens. You know the type: full of indecision, convinced that whatever they do will lead to losses.

As Buffy the Bear calmly watched Chicken Little running past yelling "The sky is falling, the sky is falling," she turned to Tabasco the Bull and whispered "Sell sky."

It takes all types to make the markets work.

I don't know about you, but my crystal ball doesn't work very well. In fact, I have as yet found no market guru whose crystal ball works very well, either. With this in mind, I long ago determined to be a follower of the markets, since it was pretty certain I would not ever lead the markets. I'll examine some "following" techniques in the technical analysis chapters of this book, as well as conduct a quick brush-up on technical analysis tools.

It may seem like there is never a right time to enter your first trade. Then again, there is probably never a wrong time. I've heard it said that throwing darts is as effective an entry method as any; you just need good money management techniques.

No matter when you first begin trading, you will experience losses. Managing your losses is what trading is all about. In this book we will discuss money management techniques and measurements of success you can use to minimize losses and maximize returns.

Before getting into the arena of money management, one must first discover ways to make the money one wants to manage. Everything in life has its mathematical component. As a mathematician, I focus on those components and amplify the role they play in my life. Therefore, when I conjure up methods for trading the markets, I invariably come up with mechanical methods. Mechanical techniques will be discussed throughout this book.

If you believe that an intuitive approach to the markets is best and that mechanical methods don't work, you are reading the wrong book—unless you want to be convinced otherwise.

Trading 101—How to Trade Like a Pro was an introduction to trading in general, hopefully answering some of your basic questions, helping you decide if you are even interested in becoming a trader, and opening up new avenues for you to pursue. *Trading 102—Getting Down to Business* will take you quickly into the mechanics of designing, testing, and implementing your own trading methodologies.

If you want to do the research, you can put together ten or twelve books and cover these subjects. I want to do something different by bringing this information together in one cohesive guide, so you won't have to do all the work I did. If the pursuit of knowledge fascinates you like it does me, use this book as a starting point, acquire the other books to which I refer, and go on from there. One can never learn enough.

That said, keep in mind that the main goal of trading is to make money. Sure, we want to enjoy the process, maintain our ethical standards, and relish the challenge, but we can do those things without making money. Be careful not to sabotage your efforts. There are many aspiring traders who spend the rest of their trading careers developing systems and observing the markets, never getting down to the primary goal of making money.

There's nothing wrong with having a career of academic research, don't get me wrong. But, if your goal is to make a profit through trading, there comes a time when you must accept that no system is perfect, no trader is perfect, and most successful traders lose more often than they win. This book will help you get on with it.

2 TECHNICAL ANALYSIS REVIEW

It is not the goal of this book to teach you all there is to know about technical analysis. I assume you already are familiar with the basic concepts and techniques. If you need to brush up on technical analysis specifics, consult one or more of the following excellent sources:

- *Technical Analysis of the Futures Markets* by John Murphy
- *The Encyclopedia of Technical Market Indicators* by Colby & Meyers
- *Trading Systems and Methods, 3rd edition* by Perry Kaufman
- *The Technical Analysis of Stocks, Options & Futures* by William Eng

I will, however, use moving averages in my discussions of testing. So, to insure that all of us are singing from the same hymnal, I'll spend just a bit of time discussing calculating moving averages.

Every design and testing concept addressed in this book is applicable to any type of technical analysis. Whether you decide to use moving averages, stochastics, oscillators, patterns, or channels (or anything else you can dream up) the techniques in this book are of general applicability. Testing is testing, whatever the hypothesis.

Technical Analysis vs. Fundamental Analysis

Technical analysis is the study of past prices; fundamental analysis is the study of reports. Fundamental analysts buy companies. Technical analysts buy stock.

There are a great many arguments for the use of fundamental analysis; I've heard them all. Everything has a time and a place. The place for using fundamental analysis is with commodities that behave according to fundamentals. For instance, natural gas prices go up just before winter—it's about to get cold and gasoline vendors can maximize profits. Gas prices go down just after winter, to encourage the public to continue using the products, and then the price goes up again just as we begin our vacations in the summer. Pretty fundamental.

Stocks, and especially stock indices, behave more predictably if you watch price than if you watch reports. Reports are generated in mahogany-filled boardrooms, by people whose job it is to make the company look its best. No board of directors likes to issue an unfavorable report; that would mean they haven't done their job of directing the company well.

Annual and quarterly reports are created by artists and printed on very glossy paper. That in itself should tell you something. It's meant to impress you.

By the time the data from a company's actual performance reaches the directors, it is old data. They then massage the data into presentable hyperbole, which is then sent to the artists, the printer, and finally to you. That sort of fundamental information is too old for me.

As a contrary indicator, the *Wall Street Journal* is exceptionally useful. But, as a purveyor of current information, it is less than useful. By the time an economic trend reaches the headlines of the *Journal,* it's over. Remember this with caution the next time you see a headline reading anything like "Dow Jones about to crash. Investors panic." That is probably a great buying opportunity.

To my mind, all the information I need to know is reflected in price. Perhaps your house is "worth" a million dollars. Maybe it "should" sell for a million dollars. But, the true value of the house is established by the buyers. If your house is up for sale at a million dollars asking price, and the only offers you get are for $600,000, then what is the house "worth?" It's worth what it sells for—no more, no less.

Likewise, a stock or a commodity is only worth what someone is willing to pay for it. All the reports in the world, telling me what a company's stock is worth, how much money they have on the books, and how bright the future looks, do not influence my trading one bit. All I want to know is what is the current selling price.

Trading a hundred shares in my little account won't move the markets. Folks like Paul Tudor Jones, John Henry, and Monroe Trout move the markets, buying and selling many thousands of contracts at a time. They have full-blown research teams and computer analysis happening faster than you or I could blink. Consequently, what they are paying, with all their inside information and analysis, is what I want to pay. I want to ride on the coattails of the "big boys" as they move the markets. My technical analysis of price action is the only thing that tells me what the big boys are doing. Follow along with a moving average. It's not sophisticated, but it works.

Curve Fitting

Often, and especially in the case of the markets, one cannot prove or disprove theories by proposing simple mathematical or logical equations. In a situation like this, I resort to empirical techniques and prove theories by experimentation. The downfall of this method is the propensity toward curve-fitting.

Definition:

Curve-Fitting
Developing complicated rules that map known conditions.

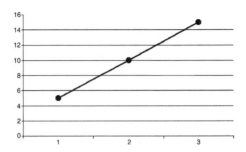

Figure 2.1 Three Data Points

In other words, if I develop enough rules, I can completely describe the current set of data. Chances are, however, that these rules will not correctly describe any future data.

A street map is a representation of the configuration of streets with respect to each other and to the surrounding land. The map is not the streets, it is just a representation of the streets.

Likewise, a map of three data points, prices in our case, is a representation of the data and is not the data itself.

A straight line can represent the three points in Figure 2.1. The problem we run into with curve fitting can be easily illustrated by adding in a fourth data point, as shown in Figure 2.2. In this case, the straight line no longer fits the data.

In Figure 2.3 we have a chart of the markets as represented by the S&P 500.

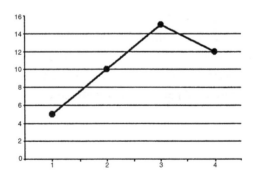

Figure 2.2 Four Data Points

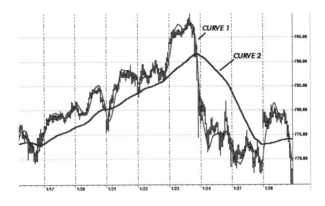

Figure 2.3   S&P 500

There are two curves in Figure 2.3, one of which is tightly fit to the data, and one which is not. Curve 1 is a linear regression curve that very closely approximates the actual data. While it looks very accurate, the chances of it fitting future data, with the same values as originally input, are slight. Curve 2 is a long-term (50 period) simple moving average of the data. Analysis based on Curve 2 is more likely to continue to be valid over time, as it is not curve-fit to the data.

What Is Your Goal?

The challenge for you as a trader is to make money, not to invent the Holy Grail indicator. Your challenge is not against other minds, to show who's the smartest, but against the zero-sum game of trading—who ends up with the most money. As the saying goes: "Whoever ends up with the biggest pile of toys wins."

Enjoy your toys, of course; never lose sight of your *raison d'etre*. But don't forget that the goal of trading is to win.

As an individual trader, you're not likely to end up with the largest pile of money, but you want to end up with a pile that will support your musts, your wants, and your hobbies, with money left to put away for a rainy day.

Predicting the Future

Again, what is your goal? Profit! To make money, not to outsmart the market. I believe that you cannot predict the future, but you can analyze the extremely recent past quickly.

Ed Seykota (see Appendix F) says that if you want to know everything about the market, go to the beach. Push and pull your hands with the waves. Some are bigger waves, some are smaller. But if you try to push the wave out when it's coming in, it'll never happen. The market is always right.

Sunny Harris says that following the market is like dancing backward with your eyes closed. Follow gracefully, but never try to lead the market.

Necessary and Sufficient Tools

To be well-defined, a system must state all the necessary steps and yet only the steps sufficient to uniquely define the procedure. In mathematics this is called "necessary and sufficient." Basically it means that you do everything you have to without overkill.

If a moving average crossover is all that is necessary to have a profitable trading method, why go any further? If I need to use a moving average and a second indicator, like momentum or stochastics to be profitable, then the moving average is necessary but not sufficient. Only by using both indicators would the necessary and sufficient conditions be met.

The foremost necessary condition is that the system makes a profit. How do I know that it will make a profit? Testing, of course. Simplistically, if a system is more likely to win than to lose over long periods of time, it has a positive mathematical expectation. If a system has a positive mathematical expectation, one can reasonably expect that it will be profitable over the long-term.

In Chapter 9, Formulae for Systems Development, I discuss the formula and procedures used for determining whether your system has a positive mathematical expectation. There I will be more specific about how you can make these calculations.

No system is fail-proof. Furthermore, no system works all the time. In every case one must suffer the losses, while keeping them small, to reap the long-term rewards. In *Mathematics of Money Management* on page 42, Ralph Vince states:

> *Chapter 1 showed that you must have a positive mathematical expectation or ruin is certain. However, of the two, systems and money management, the money management is far and away more important in terms of your performance as a trader or fund manager.*

I cannot emphasize this concept strongly enough. What this says to me is "don't give up too soon." And by all means don't give up when you're in drawdown.* If you've done all your homework, you'll expect these inevitable periods of loss and learn to accept them as a "cost of doing business."

While it is necessary that your system be profitable, that alone is not sufficient for most people. For instance, a system which makes 100 trades, where 95 of them are losers and 5 of them produce high enough wins to yield the entire process profitable, does not make most people feel very comfortable. That would be a 5 percent winning system and carry with it a great deal of psychological discomfort.

So, another necessary condition would be to impose your loss tolerance level on the system's performance by specifying the win to loss ratio. While I can comfortably trade a 35 percent winning system (35 wins to 65 losses), not everyone can. Some people are only willing to trade a 65 percent winning system.

Keep in mind that as you impose more conditions you begin to restrict other things that happen in your system. The more freedom your methodology has to flow with changing market conditions, the more likely it is to continue working in the future.

---

*Drawdown is the reduction in account equity as a result of a trade or series of trades. For an in-depth explanation, see *Trading 101—How to Trade Like a Pro,* page 128.

How Do You Prove Something?

Inductive reasoning is the use of specific facts to form a general conclusion. *Deductive reasoning* is the use of general information to form specific conclusions. In creating a trading system you will use both types of reasoning. You will deduce from your overall view of markets some specifics you believe to be true. From these specifics you will attempt to make generalizations which hold true both in historical situations and in future situations.

You will stare at a chart for hours, repeatedly asking yourself "what is true?" You will not be able to answer your question with a solid 100 percent answer like "the market *always* does . . . ," because the market doesn't. However, you will be able to statistically evaluate your chances of observing a pattern which repeats x percent of the time. When x is large enough, you've found something that's "true" of the market.

Dancing with the Market

Our goal is to make money, not to outsmart the market. Right? In Chapter 4 I'll address exactly how to do that, through the use of PHW—Potential Hourly Wage analysis. For now, put pencil to paper and do a few technical analysis calculations which will assist you when you get to that chapter.

A *Simple Moving Average* is the sum of prices (P) divided by the number of prices you used in the sum (N). It shows the average value over the specified period of time. Expressed mathematically, each subsequent moving average value is calculated from the previous N values:

$$A_i = [P_i + P_{(i-1)} \cdots + P_{(i-N+1)}]/N$$

For the remainder of the calculations in this chapter I will refer to the data in Figure 2.4. Let's take a look at it in spreadsheet format.

The chart of the simple moving averages from columns C and D is shown in Figure 2.5. The line that is consistently further away from the data is the 25-period moving average. The line that more tightly fits the data is the 5-period moving average.

A *Smoothed Moving Average* is often used by programmers as an approximation for moving averages of other types because its equations are easy to program. Be wary of any software that substitutes this shortcut in its calculations.

A	B	C	D	E	F	G	H
		Simple MAV		Smoothed MAV		Exponential MAV	
Date	Close	5 period	25 period	5 period	25 period	5 period	25 period
950103	459.11			459.11	459.11	459.11	459.11
950104	460.71			459.91	459.91	460.18	460.18
950105	460.34			460.05	460.05	460.26	460.26
950106	460.68			460.21	460.21	460.43	460.43
950109	460.83	460.33		460.33	460.33	460.59	460.56
950110	461.68	460.85		460.60	460.56	461.02	460.88
950111	461.66	461.04		460.81	460.72	461.28	461.08
950112	461.64	461.30		460.98	460.83	461.42	461.20
950113	465.97	462.36		461.98	461.40	463.24	462.15
950116	469.38	464.07		463.46	462.20	465.70	463.47
950117	470.05	465.74		464.78	462.91	467.44	464.57
950118	469.72	467.35		465.77	463.48	468.35	465.36
950119	466.95	468.41		466.00	463.75	467.79	465.59
950120	464.78	468.18		465.76	463.82	466.59	465.48
950123	465.81	467.46		465.77	463.95	466.28	465.52
950124	465.86	466.62		465.79	464.07	466.11	465.56
950125	467.44	466.17		466.12	464.27	466.64	465.77
950126	468.32	466.44		466.56	464.50	467.31	466.04
950127	470.39	467.56		467.32	464.81	468.54	466.47
950130	468.51	468.10		467.56	464.99	468.53	466.67
950131	470.42	469.02		468.13	465.25	469.29	467.01
950201	470.40	469.61		468.59	465.48	469.73	467.30
950202	472.78	470.50		469.43	465.80	470.95	467.76
950203	478.64	472.15		471.27	466.34	474.03	468.63
950206	481.14	474.68	466.93	473.24	466.93	476.87	469.59
950207	480.81	476.75	467.80	474.76	467.48	478.45	470.45
950208	481.19	478.91	468.62	476.04	468.03	479.54	471.23
950209	480.19	480.39	469.41	476.87	468.52	479.80	471.97
950210	481.46	480.96	470.24	477.79	469.04	480.47	472.70
950213	481.65	481.06	471.07	478.56	469.54	480.94	473.39
950214	482.55	481.41	471.91	479.36	470.06	481.58	474.09
950215	484.54	482.08	472.82	480.40	470.64	482.77	474.89
950216	485.22	483.08	473.77	481.36	471.22	483.75	475.69
950217	481.97	483.19	474.41	481.48	471.65	483.04	476.17
950221	482.74	483.40	474.94	481.73	472.10	482.92	476.68
950222	485.07	483.91	475.54	482.40	472.62	483.78	477.32
950223	486.91	484.38	476.23	483.30	473.19	485.03	478.06
950224	488.11	484.96	477.08	484.26	473.78	486.26	478.83
950227	483.81	485.33	477.84	484.17	474.19	485.28	479.22
950228	487.39	486.26	478.70	484.82	474.71	486.12	479.84
950301	485.65	486.37	479.49	484.98	475.15	485.93	480.29
950302	485.13	486.02	480.20	485.01	475.55	485.61	480.66
950303	485.42	485.49	480.88	485.09	475.94	485.54	481.03

Figure 2.4 *Moving Average Calculations*

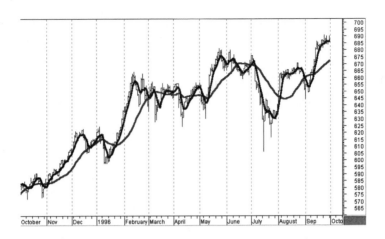

Figure 2.5   A Fast and a Slow Moving Average

A smoothed moving average begins with a starting value, often the first simple moving average, and multiplies it by $(N - 1)$, adds the current price value (P_i) and divides the total by N. Mathematically this would look like:

$$A_i = \{[A_{(i-1)} * (N - 1)] + P_i\}/N$$

Column E, in the spreadsheet in Figure 2.4, contains values calculated by the smoothed moving average method, and is shown in the chart in Figure 2.5.

Exponential Moving Averages (EMAVs) are calculated by applying a percentage of the current price (P) to the previous price's exponential moving average value. EMAVs place more important on recent prices and less on data in the past. For that reason, an EMAV will move more in concert with current market conditions than would a simple moving average.

Exponential moving averages are calculated using either a percentage weighting factor (α), or using the number of time periods (N) over which the values are calculated. Equations A and B are mathematically equivalent.

A. $$A_{i+1} = (\alpha * P_i) + [(1 - \alpha) * A_i]$$
where α is the percentage weighting

or

B. $A_{i+1} = A_i + (2/(N + 1) * (P_i - A_i))$
           where N is the number of time periods.

Figure 2.6 shows all three types of moving averages discussed here. There are more types, by the way, but you can read about those in books intended to be more technical than this one.

Which one should you use? I don't know. It all depends on your own individual design and testing. Different techniques work better in different markets. The moving average values that work on soybeans will not necessarily be the same values that work in the S&P. True, the concept will be the same: moving averages; but the input values may vary. If you see trading markets as dancing to music (as I do) then soybeans might be a waltz, while the S&P is a tango, but they're both still music.

I use modified exponential moving averages in my work. The EMAV will usually turn faster than the other types of averages; in fact, at times it turns too fast. Adding an indicator as a filter over the EMAV can act to ignore some of the turns that are too fast.

Before going on to another very important technical indicator, take a look at how the value you use for the length of the indicator can affect how closely it follows the market. There are three EMAVs on Figure 2.7, with lengths of 5, 10, and 15, respectively.

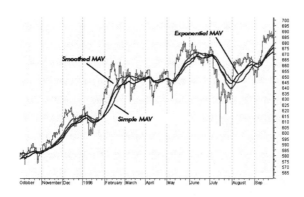

Figure 2.6   Types of Moving Averages

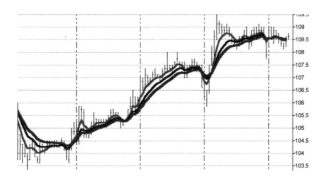

Figure 2.7 *Three Exponential Moving Averages*

Notice that as the length of the exponential moving average increases from 5 to 10 to 15, the smoothed line moves farther away from the actual data. The equation for the longer exponential moving average would be more likely to continue to model future data than would the equation for the shortest exponential moving average.

Is That All There Is?

Is a moving average "necessary"? Yes, in my work it is. Is it "sufficient"? Probably not. I like to add a confirming indicator and a denying indicator as filters on my main indicator. The resultant is a three-indicator system. The moving average crossover sets up the entry for a trade. But that's not enough to complete a profitable system.

To reduce market whipsaws, wait for confirmation from the second indicator before entering the market. The moving average tells us that the market has changed direction, but during periods of sideways market action the moving averages will cross back and forth over each other several times. Rather than take a losing trade with each of those crossovers, it makes sense to wait for confirmation that the market is trending before reversing our position or entering another trade.

There are several indicators which reveal trendiness: momentum, channel breakouts, and ADX to name a few. A good book to study regarding the use of these and more technical indicators is William Eng's *The Technical Analysis of Stocks, Options & Futures*. Again, only your testing will uncover the combination that suits your application.

In addition to evaluating the combination of entry setup and confirming indicators you might want to consider requiring that the confirmation pass a threshold before entering a trade. For instance, if the moving averages have crossed over and momentum is positive, you might require that momentum be greater than 10 before you consider it a valid confirmation.

Sometimes I use a third indicator to pinpoint excessive market conditions. Since moving averages, even exponential ones, are lagging indicators, they are by nature slower than the price action that is taking place. In cases where the market is moving rapidly, a moving average system will often get you into the move too late. If the market makes a fast run up, you'll be buying at or near the top. Rather than incur losses of this nature, I can implement a denying indicator to keep me out of overbought and oversold conditions. RSI, stochastics, and the slope of trendlines can serve this purpose. Again, refer to William Eng's (see Appendix F) book for explanations of these indicators, and test them in combinations and with varying parameters.

3   MECHANICAL TRADING SYSTEMS

Systematic Trading

Traders who are consistently successful, whether they know it or not, are using some sort of system to make trades.

A system is simply a recipe, a map, a guide that you follow to its conclusion. Your system might be as simple as trading on the long side on sunny days and on the short side on rainy days. That's a system! And if you follow that plan day after day, keeping track of the results, you can call yourself a disciplined trader.

The fear of the word "system" is like the fear of math. Usually people who didn't like math in school simply didn't have a good teacher. Likewise, if you hesitate at the word "system," it's probably for lack of a good teacher. Fear not; remember that a system is just a recipe, and you use recipes all the time.

Do you type? You are following a recipe for pressing a key that causes a particular letter to appear on the paper. Do you watch television? You follow a recipe regarding time and channel in order to view the programs you like.

Most often, the people who resist delineating the rules of their system are the people who are afraid to find out that their system doesn't work. These traders are definitely "into wishing," hoping that they will be lucky and the system will produce profits just because they deserve it.

As a mathematician and programmer, my view of the world is based in symbolic logic, and IF . . . THEN statements. I'm a strong believer in cause and effect. Thus, as a trader, I view the markets in a systematic fashion, with mathematical definition. Decision trees (IF this happens, THEN this will follow, but IF the other happens, THEN something else will follow) rooted in mathematics are the basis for my trading.

Some may say that they trade on intuition, and that's their method. My premise is that intuition is based on an unconscious set of rules, and that those rules can be translated to a computer program. Those who already trade with a set of clearly defined rules can immediately translate them to a computer program.

IF it's skill that generates the profits, THEN whether consciously or unconsciously, the trader has a set of rules in mind. IF the trade is following rules, THEN the system can be tested and verified.

I have met many traders who test their rules by hand, that is, with paper and pencil and sometimes a calculator. There is nothing wrong with that. This method is very time consuming, however, and the tendency is to give up after testing only a small subset of the data. Further, I find the hand testing method to be prone to two types of error: wishful thinking and calculation error. Calculation error is obvious: one makes a simple arithmetic mistake. Wishful thinking goes like this: "Oh, I would have taken that trade, even though this system doesn't show it." It's akin to outsmarting the system but is more subtle.

Another frequently used method of testing one's system is through the use of a spreadsheet program, such as Lotus 1-2-3, Excel, or QuattraPro. In the beginning of my trading experience, that is exactly what I did. And in fact, I still use spreadsheets to verify the accuracy of test results from other computer programs. The limitation with this method is the amount of data a spreadsheet will handle as well as the convenience and clarity of the output.

Computer testing of systems is very much like running a scientific experiment. Hypotheses are generated, assumptions are made, and the experiment is set up so as not to prejudice the results toward the bias of the tester.

Mechanical Systems

As we extend artificial intelligence techniques into every aspect of our daily lives, from automated gasoline pumps to automated bank teller machines, we also venture into automated investing.

The natural extension of creating a system is to have a computer trade it for you. I can hear it now, many of you are saying that trading would be no fun if the computer did it. Listen to yourself. Is fun what this business is about? Isn't the goal to turn a profit? I found long ago that the best way to be disciplined about my system was to specify the rules and let someone else place the trades. Don't get me wrong, I like to have fun and it's imperative that we enjoy our work, but the thrill of this job should not be of a gambling nature.

If you have sufficiently specified your rules such that someone else can trade the system, then it is a mechanical system. If you rely on intuition and feeling about the market to make your trades, chances are you can't pinpoint it enough to completely specify the rules. This type of trading is nonmechanical, and specific to the psyche of the person doing the trading. One of the pitfalls is that one's psyche can change based on mood and environment.

While mechanical traders can feel that a computer can replace them, discretionary traders maintain the illusion of job security—at least as long as they keep winning.

Do You Even Need a System?

A plan—that's all a system is. A way to go. A map. A recipe.

We use maps to travel to new cities, we use recipes to cook new dishes, and we read the instructions on a new piece of electronic equipment. These are all *systems*.

The elements of fear and trepidation come in when we introduce foreign sounding words like algorithm, methodology, and procedure. It's only your emotion reacting. A system is just a plan.

One of the great old mottos is: "Plan Your Work and Work Your Plan." That's just another way of saying "follow your system."

Don't be afraid of the word system. It's just a word. Whether you verbalize it or not, you already have an investment or trading plan. If you look at the ticker tape, if you read prices from the newspaper, if you're looking at a computer to get your prices, somehow you've analyzed what you see and interpreted it to a plan of action. Whether you've realized it or not, you already have a system.

You may think your trading is completely discretionary and that you are an intuitive trader. I disagree! Anything you do is composed of small signals sent by your brain to your muscles. Each signal, given enough tedium and concentration, can be translated to words, and those words are the program your brain executes.

The challenge, therefore, is to document the procedure you follow, so that someone else can follow it. I don't mean by this that you should give away your secrets; I simply mean for you to create a written procedure so you'll know when you are cheating. And you know when you really know.

What do you look at? What if you are discretionary or intuitive? You still have criteria that you examine. Even if you close your eyes and throw darts, you have a procedure. Each time you begin the evaluation process before pulling the trigger, you follow the same steps.

In order for you to consistently follow the procedure, it must be defined. If your procedure is defined only in your head, human nature will intervene and you will falter. Get your recipe down on paper. Have it beside you so that you evaluate each step before taking a trade. Soon the evaluation process will become as natural as stepping on the brake in your car—it will be rapid and seem to you that you are no longer evaluating each step of the process individually.

It is difficult for many people to grasp just how to specify their system. A lot of hand waving goes along with most systems. Many systems, even commercial ones, will give you entry points and leave you on your own when it's time to choose an exit. That's only half a system. Each and every step along the way must be specified before a system is "well-defined."

In our seminars, which develop both right- and left-brain skills, Adrienne Toghraie and I give a little demonstration which illustrates the nature of specifying one's system. Starting with a plate, a knife, a bag of sliced bread, a jar of jelly, and a jar of peanut butter, we ask each participant to write down the recipe for a peanut butter and jelly sandwich, exactly. We get a few guffaws, and the participants begin to write. In a large group, several people will be precise in their details, leading us carefully through the procedure with their instructions, but most of the recipes make many assumptions. At the end of five minutes, we ask for the recipes and choose one to demonstrate. Often the process of demonstrating the "system" becomes a messy one, fraught with oversights and assumptions.

For instance, here's an example of the type of recipe we see often:

Take the peanut butter and put it on the bread. Put the jelly on the peanut butter. Eat the sandwich.

If you'll take a second to visualize this one, the result is a jar of jelly atop a jar of peanut butter resting on top of a sealed loaf of bread. No one wanted to try to eat that one.

In another example a student specified most of the steps correctly, but forgot to instruct us to use the knife. As directed, we took the peanut butter out of the jar, without using the knife.

To be well-defined, a system must state **all** the necessary steps and **only** the steps sufficient to uniquely define the procedure. In mathematics we call this "necessary and sufficient." A well-defined recipe might go like this:

Open the bag of bread, removing one slice and placing it on the table, face up. Pick up the jar of peanut butter with your left hand. Remove the lid with your right hand, turning the top counterclockwise. Place the lid on the table. Pick up the knife with your right hand. Place the knife into the jar of peanut butter, scooping out approximately one tablespoon of peanut butter. Place the jar of peanut butter on the table. Spread the peanut butter, which is on the knife, onto the slice of bread which is laying face up on the table. Lay the knife temporarily on the table. Pick up the jar of jelly with your left hand. Remove the lid with your right hand, turning the top counterclockwise. Place the lid on the table. Pick up the knife with your right hand. Place the knife into the jar of jelly, scooping out approximately one tablespoon of jelly. Place the jar of jelly on the table. Spread the jelly, which is on the knife, onto the peanut butter which is on the slice of bread which is laying face up on the table. Lay the knife on the table. Remove one slice of bread from the bag of bread. Place the bread squarely atop the bread which has been spread with jelly and peanut butter.

Granted, that's tedious. But it's well-defined. Still, there are many other recipes for making the same sandwich with the same materials.

Whenever you think about trading from now on, remember the peanut butter and jelly sandwich. Ask yourself if you're really doing all your homework, or if you're skipping steps. Skipped steps often result in error.

In the past you may have thought you created a peanut butter and jelly sandwich by intuition or "feel." Now you know that you have been following a procedure, which you've done so many times that it has become intuitive.

The same can be true of successful trading. If you've been watching the markets for many years, and you just seem to "know" what it's going to do next, you may be letting your subconscious process all the steps without ever raising the system to your conscious level. But if you want to be a systematic trader, and if you want to give your trading the benefit of rigorous proof, then you'll need to specify all the steps.

True, you may have difficulty describing each and every step, but your trading is not arbitrary. The rules are there. Somehow you notice in your subconscious that a similar thing happens over and over in the market, and when it does you take action. If you are an "intuitive" trader, you must recognize that you are seeing or feeling something in the market that causes you to take action.

I am not advocating that every trading system be turned into a mechanical, computerized automation. I am, however, suggesting that for your neurology to trust you, you must give it proof. You must give it reason to believe that you consistently win over time. Otherwise, your neurology will step quickly into fear mode, and you will experience doubt and panic as you view losing trades. If you have papers which show the statistics of your trading, proving that in the long run you make profits, you are less likely to get into the immobilizing crater of doubt that most traders experience.

Banks and institutions often frown upon the word "system." Upper management asks, "Why would I hire a trader if I have a system?" The value of a trader in an institutional setting is that there are an infinite number of systems, not just a few. A banker wouldn't loan you money for a new business without a business plan; yet a banker would hire a trader without a system. It doesn't make sense to me; I have to assume it is part of the bureaucratic mind.

Your medical doctor probably uses a computer in his office to assist in analyzing your disease based on the symptoms and differential diagnosis. His computer can instantly sort through an enormous database of possibilities, giving him a readout of analyses. The physician is still needed for the art of interpreting the cold statistics. But he has been carefully trained over many years in the science of systematic analysis.

Conversely, please don't step into the trap of trading a system blindly. Every week we get telephone calls and emails asking which system "works." People so frequently want a free lunch or a quick fix. Remember, *there is no Holy Grail.* Your trading system must be based on your personality type, and the way you interpret the events, not on someone else's. Many people want to jump into the markets quickly, and heeding the warnings about the danger of skipping the homework stage, decide to cheat off someone else's homework. Exercise caution. The homework you're cheating from may belong to the F student.

Before purchasing a trading system, test it yourself. If you don't have access to historical data, then procure a trial version of the system and test it by watching the market over the next few months, seeing how the system would perform. There are many very good systems available for purchase, and there are many systems that aren't so good.

There are many factors that can affect your conscious and subconscious emotional states, which then affect your trading. Everything from psychological and environmental changes to lunar cycles can affect your trading. As human beings we are composed largely of water. The water in the oceans is pulled into tides by the magnetic energy of the moon and the sun. In all likelihood, we too are pushed and pulled in relation to the new moons and full moons. Magnetic storms on the sun, called sunspots, not only affect our moods but also play a role in the stability of our electronic equipment.

When your electronic equipment is broken down, you usually know it. Did you ever fail to notice a hard-disk crash on your computer? The problem is, our psyches are not so easily monitored. We often don't know we've broken down, until someone close to us says we're in a bad mood. Even then, how many times have you retorted, "I am not! You are!"

More obvious than sunspot activity, we are heavily influenced by our environments. A toothache can keep you from maintaining focus. A fight with your significant other or your offspring can bring you to your knees. At times like these, you had better have your system in place, well-defined and tested, or your tendency will be to express your emotions through your trading.

It's the combination of man and machines that really works well in this business. A carefully constructed system that has been back- and forward-tested, and that meets all the criteria of a proven system (see Chapter 9), will keep you on track during the roughest times—that is, if you follow it.

Master traders will tell you that good trading is boring. The biggest excitement you'll get is in the developmental stages. When you trade for excitement you get into trouble. It is better financially for you to trade automatically and attach the emotional rewards to some other hobby in your life which does not affect your income.

Steps to Mechanization

There are four steps in any successful business plan. (See Figure 3.1.)

Likewise, there are four steps to successful trading. (See Figure 3.2.) In fact, these four steps mirror the steps of any successful business.

Naturally, each step has sub-steps, and I will describe those later. For now, let's look at the broad brushstrokes to creating a mechanical trading plan.

The business of trading involves market analysis, product creation and testing, and product sales, just like any other business. In the case of trading for yourself, however, the product sales stage is your actual trading effort. This is the phase that (hopefully) brings in the money.

Much like the creation of any product, there are stages to its development and testing, before you let it loose on the unsuspecting public. In this case, if you are developing a system for your-

Step 1: Market Analysis	Step 2: Product Creation	Step 3: Quality Assurance	Step 4: Sales

Figure 3.1 Steps to a Successful Business

Step 1: Overview Analysis	Step 2: System Design	Step 3: Testing	Step 4: Trading

Figure 3.2 Steps to Successful Trading

self, *you* are the unsuspecting public. If you go into production mode without adequate testing and system verification, you will suffer the consequences of an unproven trading system: loss.

Overview Analysis—Step 1

Establishing a sensible overview of the possibilities involves taking a broad look at the markets and determining which one or ones fit your style and at the same time will make you money.

The first question I pose when beginning any business endeavor is, will it make money? If so, how much money? And with how much effort?

Jumping blindly into a new business, hoping it will make you a lot of money because you heard the success stories of other traders, is not a good way to start.

With any business, you want to create and analyze your balance sheet. What is the potential income? What are the likely expenses? Having determined the overview, it's always a more realistic approach *to reduce the expected income by half and double the expenses.* If the balance sheet still looks good after that, continue with the analysis.

Since it is really true that a picture is worth a thousand words, I like to conduct my research using charts whenever possible. Step 1, the Overview Analysis, lends itself nicely to just such an endeavor.

Systems Design—Step 2

Your second step is to take the rough sketches you've made in Step 1 and implement them. Your first implementation will not be a trading system. It will be merely a prototype. Envision yourself as an inventor in this process. As you devise your new methods you will encounter lots of situations in which your invention doesn't work. Be patient. Steps 2 and 3 require an enormous amount of time and energy.

Ninety percent of all new startup businesses fail. Ninety percent of an inventor's ideas fail. Ninety percent of a professional photographer's pictures are throwaways. And ninety percent of the ideas you test while designing your system will not work out.

If there were a get-rich-quick scheme, everyone would be doing it.

Testing—Step 3

Steps 2 and 3 go hand in hand. It is difficult to separate the initial idea generation from the testing, because each prototype you mold will require a certain amount of testing to generate the failure conditions.

As mathematicians we are trained to look for the counter examples. While you often can't prove the existence of something, you can prove that it doesn't exist. You can't prove that your system will always work, but you can prove that it will fail. View the failures as being just one step closer to finding the successes.

Each time you come up with a possible candidate for review you will test it over a sample of your data to determine whether to continue in this vein or to eliminate the pathway. This part of the testing step is short in duration and intended only to "separate the wheat from the chaff."

The bulk of the testing phase consists of subjecting your prototypes to rigorous tests both to discover potential pitfalls and to refine and optimize the prototype into a shiny working model. We will discuss the procedures of testing and recommend specific methods later on in this book.

Trading—Step 4

This is the part you're waiting for. Hopefully you are waiting and not jumping in before you finish studying and conducting your research. Trading before you've completed Steps 1–3 most often results in severe reductions of capital, meaning you will run out of money before you really learn what you should be doing.

The actual trading process should be the least strenuous and least time-consuming part of your job. The more you can prepare in advance, the less stressful trading will be.

Trading should simply be a matter of following the steps you've set forth in Step 3 and keeping track of the results.

Setting and Following the Rules

Some of the best systems go against traditional or intuitive rules. The proof is in the testing. You might find that your stockbroker's advice of "buy and hold" is not the best advice for a trader. You might find that trading only on Mondays works for you. Don't be afraid to brainstorm and then experiment.

Flying in the Face of Tradition

Some of the adages that you'll hear often as a trader are very well founded and some are simply not true. How will you know which is which? Testing, my friend; find out for yourself through diligent experimentation.

One saying which immediately comes to mind is: never take a loss home. This means that you should not hold onto a losing trade overnight. Why not? Don't all trades go up and down in the course of the trade? Have you ever seen a trade that just goes up linearly? Have you ever seen a trade that loses in the beginning, only to make a great profit before it's closed? We call the movement that is against our desired direction an *adverse excursion*.

What about the example in Figure 3.3—a trade on the S&P 500 futures? The circled area shows where we went long, at 785. By the end of that day, the trade was in a small losing position having lost $500—an adverse excursion. The next morning, the trade became even a bit more negative in the first 15-minute period, but immediately thereafter began to gain profits. By the end of the second day the trade had 9 points profit—$4,500! On the third day profits climbed even higher, achieving a 14-point gain before turning around. Our exit reversal took us short at 792,

(SP 67/99) S&P 500 INDEX 67/99-Daily   12/16/1997 C=980.40 +6.20 +0 64% O=978.00 H=985.50 L=976.60 V=231952

Figure 3.3   A Trade with an Adverse Excursion

keeping $3,500 profit. That trade would not have happened if we followed the adage.

The only way we can refute "traditional wisdom" is to test our ideas. For instance, if your testing indicated that 70 percent of the time trades with an adverse excursion less than $500 turned into winners, you would probably want to hang tight during these episodes. Beginning with Chapter 6, I go into the mechanics of testing at great length. From there to Chapter 13 you'll learn what constitutes a proof and how to prove your own system.

The Proof Is in the Testing

How would you know whether to listen to what others tell you or to ignore the tradition? You must take the time to prove or disprove it for yourself.

In the example above, your testing routine would have several phases:

- Testing your data holding trades overnight
- Testing the same data, with the same parameters, exiting all losing trades at the end of the day
- Testing the same data with the same parameters, exiting all trades with adverse excursions larger than some fixed dollar amount

31

Be sure that you test the same conditions with the second and third tests that you generated with the first. Only through this extensive, and time-consuming, testing process will you discover which trading method is best.

The Outcome Is the Result of Your Implementation

The system can't trade itself. How you implement it will govern the success or failure of the outcome.

Probably the most difficult part of trading is in maintaining discipline. Whether you purchase a system from someone, or design and prove it yourself, chances are you won't follow every trade it recommends.

How can I say this? Because I've talked with and observed thousands of traders, some novices and some veterans. Very, very few of them take every trade their system takes.

You might have the best system in the world, and still there will be times when you choose to "outsmart" it. Or, maybe you decide to take a vacation and travel for a week or two. As soon as you miss even one trade that the system takes, you are no longer implementing the system, by definition.

Your outcome is dependent on how closely your implementation resembles the theoretical system. I judge my success (given a proven system, of course) on how close I am to the system's theoretical results. I continually track both the theoretical results and the actual results, trade by trade.

Successful Implementation Comes from a Neurologically Balanced Trader

The balanced trader is one who has successfully integrated right-brain thinking with left-brain thinking. Your right brain controls your left hand, and your left brain controls your right hand. Have you ever noticed the abundance of artists and actors who are left-handed? It stands to reason, since the right brain controls creativity. If you are a left-brained, structured, logical person, you will want to enhance your right-brain skills, becoming more creative. Conversely, if you are predominantly right-brained, emotional, and creative, you will want to tackle the structured aspects of your life.

When you have cultivated your ability to use both sides of your brain you will be both intuitive and logical. Balancing your neurology facilitates your system's design and testing, as well as your ability to consistently follow your methodology.

One of my problematic traders is very consistent about following the system inconsistently. This trader shows good intent, saying he will take each and every signal "from now on" only to fade out when the going gets tough. His intention is good, as he prepares systematically and psychologically, but his follow-through is lacking. I can't do it for him; only he can modify his thinking and acting so that he will become more confident.

With a properly tested and proven system, when it gets into drawdown, you must continue to follow its signals. You will not know when the system is ready to jump into profitability mode again, and it often does with a vengeance. The trade you miss by second-guessing is typically the one which more than makes up for the drawdown period. Second-guessing your system by attempting to avoid the losing trades doesn't work. The only way to avoid taking losing trades based on the performance of previous trades is if your system is "dependent."

If you would like to know how the concept of dependency translates mathematically, take a look at Ralph Vince's work. Vince discusses dependence and independence in each of his books.* Suffice it to say that only if a system is dependent can you profitably trade the equity curve, standing aside when the system enters drawdown. Vince's first book, *Mathematics of Money Management,* is probably best for your initial investigation of this concept.

---

*To date Ralph Vince has written *Mathematics of Money Management, Portfolio Management Formulas,* and *The New Money Management.*

Automation

One way to guarantee that you follow the system you design is to automate it. If your computer, not you, is in charge of watching the market, it won't randomly make emotional decisions based on fear or greed, or sabotage.

Programs like TradeStation by Omega Research, MetaStock by Equis, and Day Trader by Window On WallStreet allow you to precisely specify your trading plan in its internal programming language and test strategies over historical data.

TradeStation allows automation of your system to the extent that it will sound an alarm when it finds that market conditions match your specifications. If you can trust the audible alerts and ignore the minute-by-minute gyrations of the market you'll be more likely to follow your system. Better yet, you can program TradeStation to send the signal to your alphanumeric pager, so you can receive the alert to trade and not even be near your computer.

As an alternative to the computerized automated approach, let someone else place your trades for you. Having designed, tested, and clearly defined your rules, an employee or friend can make the trades for you, again avoiding emotional pitfalls. Further, there are several brokerage firms that will automatically make the trades for you, based on your rules. Clearly there is a fee for their efforts, but it may pale in comparison to your second-guessing mistakes. And it gives you the freedom to do something else besides watch a computer screen all day.

Data Collection

One of the most important components of your trading is your data. If your data is inaccurate, you will be taking unfounded trades. As in any scientific experiment, you must maintain accuracy and consistency.

Remember:

- You get what you pay for.
- Penny wise, pound foolish.

If you get your data from friends, or other free sources, you are likely to get the data you deserve. Cleaning data and guaranteeing that it is correct with actual market events is an expensive process. This process takes employees and computers both to guarantee accuracy. I know very few companies and employees who are so altruistic that they would work for free. Free doesn't buy groceries. So, if you are about to base trading decisions (which could amount to thousands of dollars in gain or loss) on the market data you acquire, make sure you've gotten it from a reliable source.

There are many companies that clean and market historical data, some of it daily data, some of it tick data, and some of it real-time. Here are just a few you can check with:

- ADP Financial Information
  Services   1-800-237-6683
- Bloomberg Financial Markets   1-212-318-2000
- Bonneville Market Information—
  BMI   1-800-255-7374
- Bridge Information Systems   1-314-567-8100
- Commodity Systems, Inc. (CSI) 1-800-274-4727
- Data Broadcasting (DBC)   1-800-367-4670
- Data Transmission Network—
  DTN   1-800-485-4000 x3330
- Dial Data   1-800-275-5544
- Dow Jones Telerate, Inc.   1-201-938-4407
- Ford Investment Services   1-800-842-0207
- FutureSource Inc.   1-800-621-2628
- Genesis Financial Data Service 1-800-808-3282
- Knight-Ridder Financial   1-800-537-9617
- PC Quote, Inc.   1-800-225-5657
- Prophet Information Services Inc. 1-800-772-8040

- Real Time Quotes Inc.   1-800-888-7166
- S&P Comstock   1-800-431-2602 x555
- Shaw Data Services   1-212-682-8877
- Stock Data Corp.   1-410-280-5533
- Telescan, Inc.   1-800-324-8246
- Tick Data, Inc.   1-800-822-8425

Lastly, don't forget to do regular backups—of your data and of your software.

4   CALCULATING YOUR POTENTIAL HOURLY WAGE™ (PHW)

Introduction

In Chapter 9 of *Trading 101—How to Trade Like a Pro* I discussed trading vehicles at length. There is no need to go over territory here that was already covered in that book.

The critical issue in deciding what to trade is: Does it make money? That is, can **you** make money trading it? Don't get married to a trading vehicle just because you like it. You must allocate the huge amount of energy you are about to expend on a worthwhile endeavor.

While you are deciding what to trade, keep in mind that you presumably have a limited amount of capital to use (or lose), and a finite amount of time you are willing to invest in the effort. It is important to optimize these two scarcest of commodities to result in the greatest personal reward.

How Much Can I Risk?

You certainly don't want to take your entire life's savings and put it into the market! That's a great way to go broke quickly.

Don't ever risk more money trading than you can afford to lose. That statement can be pretty bland, so let's look at it another way. If I gave you a $1 bill and a match, would you light the match and burn the bill or would you put it in your pocket? How about a $10 bill? How about $100? How about $1,000? How about $10,000? Are you starting to feel uncomfortable?

The level at which you are no longer comfortable with burning the bill is where your risk aversion lies. Okay, it was my money. But, what if it were actually yours? Don't ever trade beyond your level of personal comfort.

Appendix D contains a table of current margin requirements. Keep in mind that this is not the Internet, so I can't change the numbers in this book daily. By the time this gets to press it will be six months later, and the margin requirements could be very different from now. Nevertheless, by looking at this table you can get an idea of what you can afford to trade.

Clearly, if you only have $5,000 to risk, you can't trade the S&P futures contract, which currently has a $15,000 margin requirement. But you could trade soybeans, with its $1,350 margin requirement.

As we begin analyzing PHW, keep in mind your threshold for pain and the size of your pocketbook. If I'm analyzing the S&P 500 futures contract, extrapolate from that using your own parameters and make the same analysis on soybeans—or whatever.

Inflation Rears Its Ugly Head

Another consideration, which must be taken into account when trading for a living, is the affect inflation and deflation have on our true net profits. If you make $1,000 this year trading, and the cost of living goes up by $1,000 for the year, you haven't made anything. In fact, you have just put out a lot of sweat and toil (figuratively, of course) for nothing. And worse yet, taxes will take a big bite out of the $1,000, leaving you in a negative position for the year.

Our government reports that inflation is at all-time lows. Is that true? Do you believe it? Is our economy growing and expanding or is it actually contracting?

One measure of our economy's success would be how well the stock market is doing. By that measure, everyone in the United States should have nearly doubled their income in the last two years. Have you?

While our statistics may look pretty good on paper, all of us know that "figures lie and liars figure." Do you feel twice as rich as you did two years ago? I haven't talked with anyone who does. It takes two people working to support one family these days. And even then it is tough making ends meet. Have you ever wondered why?

If you adjust the DJIA to take into account spending power, you would probably get a better feeling for the reality of the situation. One way to adjust the DJIA for inflation would be to divide the year-end close of the DJIA by the Consumer Price Index (CPI), giving us a constant-dollar value for our stock market proxy. (See Figure 4.1.)

This analysis says that from 1964 until 1980 we were in a bear market, with the "real-dollar" Dow declining in value for sixteen years. Further, from 1980 to present we have been in a dramatic uptrend, which finally recovered to 1964 levels in 1995. Thus, 1996 was the first year that our standard of living had actually increased since 1964.

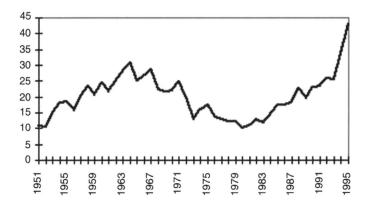

Figure 4.1 Dow Jones Industrial Average Adjusted by CPI, 1951–1996

This sounds a little more like everyone feels, doesn't it? But it is not the whole story. Are the components of the CPI the same as they were in 1950? No. Just as the components of the DJIA change with time, the CPI has been changed by the federal government's bean counters as individual components became "out of line." In other words, if the price of oil gets too high, they will remove it temporarily from the calculations. Furthermore, just as I was completing this manuscript, the components of the DJIA were changed by removing Westinghouse, Woolworth, Texaco, and Bethlehem Steel and by adding Johnson & Johnson, Hewlett-Packard, Travelers, and WalMart.

Thus, Woolworth's impending bankruptcy was not reflected in the Dow in any way.

I recently came across some numbers which may tell more of the story than the ever-changing CPI does. In Figure 4.2, you will see a tabular accounting of average values in years past. Figure 4.3 is a chart of an index created by dividing the Dow by the average annual income for that time period. We don't yet have the figures for the year 2000, but one can clearly see that the DJIA doesn't really have the parabolic upswing of Figure 4.1; adjusted for real spending power the DJIA was not much better off in 1990 than it was in 1910!

	1910	1920	1930	1940	1950	1960	1970	1980	1990
DJIA	82	90	237	134	216	610	822	946	2,633
Life Expectancy	50	54.1	59.7	62.9	68.2	69.7	70.8	73.7	75.4
Avg. Income	$1,156	$ 2,160	$1,937	$1,725	$3,216	$ 5,199	$ 9,357	$19,173	$ 28,906
New House	$3,395	$ 6,296	$7,146	$3,925	$8,450	$12,675	$23,400	$68,714	$123,000
New Car	$ 950	$ 525	$ 610	$ 850	$1,511	$ 2,610	$ 3,979	$ 7,201	$ 16,012
Loaf of Bread	$ 0.04	$ 0.12	$ 0.09	$ 0.06	$ 0.14	$ 0.20	$ 0.22	$ 0.51	$ 0.70
Gallon of Gas	$ 0.09	$ 0.13	$ 0.10	$ 0.11	$ 0.18	$ 0.26	$ 0.36	$ 1.19	$ 1.34
Gal. Milk	$ 0.34	$367.00	$ 0.56	$ 0.51	$ 0.84	$ 1.04	$ 1.32	$ 2.02	$ 2.78
Gold per oz	$20.67	$ 20.67	$20.67	$35.00	$35.00	$ 35.00	$ 36.41	$612.56	$ 386.90
Silver per oz	$ 0.54	$ 1.09	$ 1.09	$ 0.71	$ 0.90	$ 0.90	$ 1.77	$ 20.63	$ 4.80

Figure 4.2 Real Spending Power, 1951–1996

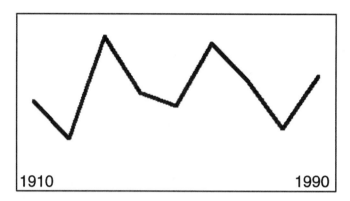

Figure 4.3   Dow Jones Industrial Average—
Adjusted by Average Income, 1910–1990

The point of these exercises was to remind you that trading is not a get rich quick scheme. It's a lot of hard work over a long period of time. Please applaud your performance whenever you are averaging 10 percent or more per year. I am not trying to dissuade you from trading, I'm just hoping you won't get discouraged if you don't make 100 percent every year.

How Much Money Can You Make?

For my own analysis I've come up with a process which I use in determining which markets are tradable. I take a look at all markets *on the same scale,* over a one-year period, and mark the ideal entries and exits from both the short and the long perspective. If 40 percent of the ideal would give me an annual wage I'd be happy with, then I consider the market to be tradable. I initially called that "Potential Hourly Wage™" Analysis (PHW Analysis), and though the concept grew well beyond hourly computations, the name stuck.

For instance, if a market only moves up an eighth and down an eighth, there is no way you can catch both of those moves. If a market moves up a point and down a point, and each point is

41

worth one dollar, you probably won't want to experiment with that one either. How many one-dollar trades would you have to take to make a respectable living?

On the other hand, if a market moves up a thousand dollars and then down a thousand dollars, you can probably catch part of that move.

Of course, the other part of the analysis is to consider over what time frame the move occurs. If it takes ten years to make that move, you'll still want to consider another market to analyze.

When analyzing any market, I consider potential monetary reward over a fixed timeframe. That's why I call it PHW. It's not that you have to get $5 per hour out of all markets, it's that you need to be able to generate a regular and predictable outcome that can be increased through multiple contracts or compounding or both.

The three steps in estimating your PHW are:

1. Marking ideal trades
2. Overview analysis
3. Accounting for reality

With every chart or new commodity you consider, always use the same comparative scales so that you are comparing apples to apples.

To fairly evaluate whether one instrument offers more trading opportunity than another, look at them both on a scale which shows equal dollar movement. For instance, if I were trying to decide whether to trade two stocks, say General Electric and IBM, I would put them on the same price scale, as in Figure 4.4.

To me GE (the lower price curve) looks like an investment opportunity, while IBM looks like a trading opportunity. GE just meanders up the scale, a little at a time, while IBM makes sharp moves upward followed by sharp moves downward.

In another arena, if I were trying to choose between trading the S&P or the T-Bonds contract, I would first have to equalize them in some way. Bonds trade at numbers around 100, seen as 99^12, 106^17, and 118^05. The carat (^) indicates that the next number is in 32nds; thus 106^17 would mean 106 and 17/32, or 106.53125.

Figure 4.4   GE and IBM

The S&P currently trades in the 600–800 range. Putting these two commodities on the same scale without equalizing them would be unfair. There is something else we must consider. On an average day the S&P will have a range between the high and the low of about 6 points, while on the same average day the bonds have a range of about ¾ point. However, the margin for the S&P is about $15,000 while the margin requirement is only approximately $3,000 for the bonds. If I traded five bond contracts for every one S&P contract, these two instruments would be performing on a more level playing field, with the reformatted bonds "unit" then moving (5) * (.75) = 3.75 points per "average" day. Furthermore, instead of being on a price scale in the 100s, the new bonds unit would be on a price scale around 500 or 600. You can see how this looks in Figure 4.5.

Step 1—Marking the Ideal Trades

In every case, the first thing I do is look at charts. Spend some time with your eyes blurred, getting a feel for the rhythm of the price activity of that chart.

The charts in Figures 4.6 through 4.13 are presented so that you may take a look at this process step by step with me. To illustrate how the concept works on several different types of trading instruments, I've chosen a commodity (coffee), an equity (IBM), the S&P 500 futures index, and a mutual fund (Templeton Growth Fund) for us to evaluate. All four charts have movement: prices trend up and then they trend down, rather than just going in one direction. All four charts are approximately a year in duration and are formed by daily data.

However, I have not initially presented all four charts to you on the same scale. This is one of those "do as I say, not as I do" situations, because I want you to scale your charts first. But if I scaled them first, you wouldn't be able to see some of the arrows once they were printed in this book, because identical scaling often flattens out some of the apparent movement.

If all four of these charts were first presented to you on identical scales, you would visually be able to recognize which ones had trading opportunity and which ones did not. In fact, looking at Figure 4.8, you can tell that there are probably more trading opportunities in the S&P than in the bonds.

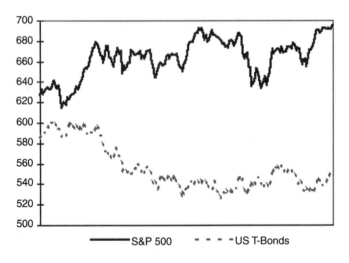

Figure 4.5 S&P 500 with Reformatted "Bonds"

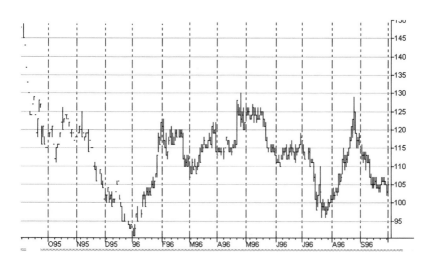

Figure 4.6 *Coffee—Ups and Downs*

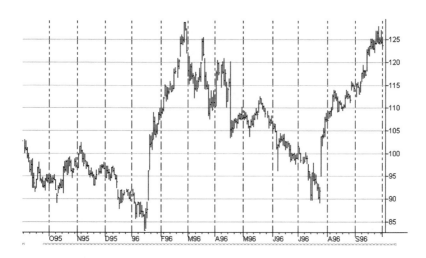

Figure 4.7 International Business Machines (IBM)—
Ups and Downs

45

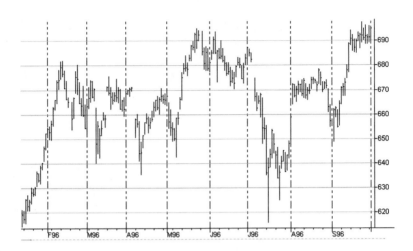

Figure 4.8   S&P 500—Ups and Downs

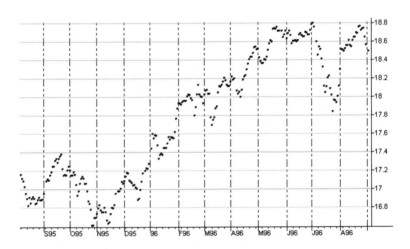

Figure 4.9   Templeton Growth Fund—Ups and Downs

Before turning the page to the charts I have marked, take out your pencil and draw arrows on these charts where you would buy and sell.

I look for peaks and valleys, not for every turn in the market. Realistically, you are not privy to the magic of the market and will make your living catching only portions of definitive moves.

Figures 4.10 through 4.13 show the way I would mark these four charts. I use an upward triangle to mark buys and a downward triangle to show sells.

How did your entry points compare to mine? Remember that this is all subjective. I didn't mark the "right" entries, and neither did you. Right and wrong are not the issues I am concerned with. Trading is more about profit than about philosophy. In fact, I don't even know yet whether the entries I have marked will be profitable. That is the next step of our analysis.

Would any of these be a good trading vehicle? This is an answer you should always know, long before you consider trading any instrument, whether it be a stock, mutual fund, or commodity.

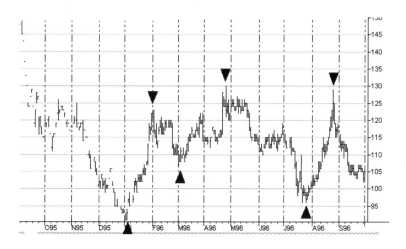

Figure 4.10 Coffee—Buy and Sell Points

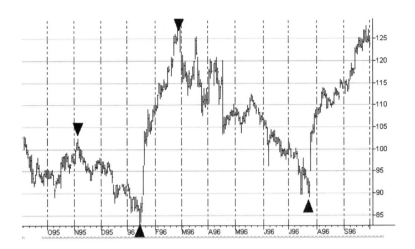

Figure 4.11 International Business Machines (IBM)—
Buy and Sell Points

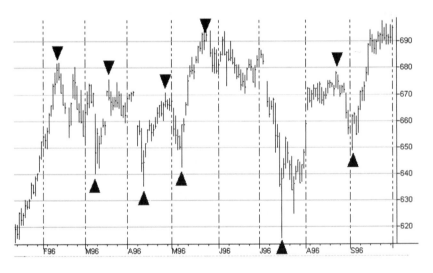

Figure 4.12 S&P 500—Buy and Sell Points

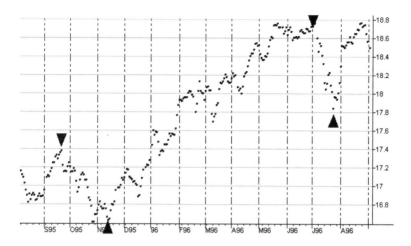

Figure 4.13 Templeton Growth Fund—Buy and Sell Points

You must compare apples to apples. Determining PHW is actually part of your business analysis. Can this business make money? And, if so, how much?

Some software products, like MetaStock, provide my PHW indicator as a built-in indicator, making your job just that much easier. If your software does not provide the PHW indicator, give my office a call at 1-888-68-SUNNY. We'll try to help.

Step 2—Overview Analysis

Now that I've marked the places I think would be good opportunities, I need to determine how well I did (or could have done). A spreadsheet like Excel or Lotus 1-2-3 or even a calculator and paper will help.

I'll do this overview in two parts. First I look at the beginning and end of the chart to see what a buy-and-hold strategy would achieve and then delve deeper to discover the trading possibilities.

A. Long Range Analysis

Using a one year chart, look to see what the range is from the lowest low of that year to the highest high of that year. Using our four charts I found the approximations shown in Figure 4.14.

Instrument	High	Low	Difference
Coffee	130	90	40
IBM	130	80	50
S&P 500	700	610	90
Templeton	19	16.6	2.4

Figure 4.14   Approximations

a. Subtracting the low from the high, what is the maximum number of points you could have made that year, viewing the instrument from a buy and hold strategy? Put the result in the "Difference" column.

b. How much is a point worth? At the time of this writing, the S&P moves in 5/100 increments, with each full point move being worth $500. Coffee moves in 5/100 increments as well, with each full point being worth $375. For the mutual fund and the stock, a point is a dollar. (See Figure 4.15.)

c. How many shares/contracts would you have to hold to make $100,000 in profits that year in each of the instruments (making the enormous assumption that you could have positioned yourself to take advantage of that range)? (See Figure 4.16.)

Now we know something concrete, as opposed to supposition.

Instrument	Difference	Point Value	Possible Profit
Coffee	40	375	15,000
IBM	50	1	50
S&P 500	90	500	45,000
Templeton	2.4	1	2.4

Figure 4.15   Possible Profits

Instrument	Possible Profit	Shares to Make $100,000
Coffee	15,000	7
IBM	50	2,000
S&P 500	45,000	3
Templeton	2.4	42,000

Figure 4.16   Shares to Make $100,000

Next we need to determine just how much money it would take to control the number of shares required to generate the ideal profit. This answer is not as concrete nor as readily determined as the numbers in the other steps.

While it is true that IBM was trading at about $95 at the beginning of our sample year, and that 2,000 shares at $95 each would be $190,000, I don't know whether you qualify to trade on margin or not, nor do I know whether you would want to if you could. Only you know your financial situation and your aversion to risk.

This same problem is even more difficult to solve when it comes to the commodities, which can be traded with very small margins. The S&P started the year at approximately 610. With its multiplier of 500, that would bring the cash value of the contract to $305,000. In Step C above, I found that I would need to trade three contracts. That would mean putting up $915,000, if I wanted to trade the S&P without leverage. That is not what most people do, of course. Usually people take advantage of the low margin requirements with these commodities, and put up the minimum amount they can trade with. Looking in Appendix D I find that the margin for the S&P is about $15,000. Trading three contracts with the minimum margin would thus mean we would need $45,000. Doubling that amount, to open the account with a safety cushion, $90,000 is still less than you would need to trade the equivalent amount of IBM. This is why futures trading seems so attractive.

However, let me remind you that futures trading is very risky because of the low margin requirements. While you only need the minimum requirement to begin trading, you are still responsible for the entire cash amount, should the market drop to zero. Compare this situation to owning a house. If you purchase a $915,000 house and have 20 percent as your down payment, you are still responsible to the mortgage company for the full mortgage if the house burns to the ground.

If you open a futures account with the minimum margin requirement and your first trade is a loss, you will have to stop trading immediately or put up more cash, since you no longer have the required minimum in your account. You will have to determine your own guidelines based on your anticipated and calculated drawdown, but my own rule of thumb is to open an account with at least double the margin requirement.

B. Short Range Analysis

Now that we have made a quick sketch of the possibilities, we can get more specific. I do the long range analysis first, because it often eliminates some trading instruments right at the onset. There is no need to go through the remainder of the calculations if something fails the first test.

Since I'm writing the book, I get to choose what instrument I will use for this next part of the analysis; of course, I'll use my favorite—the S&P 500.

Looking at its chart again, I see in Figure 4.12 that I have marked five ideal short trades and five ideal long trades on the chart. Each trade, except for the first and the last, is a reversal of the previous trade. By that I mean that if you want to trade one contract, starting from the first short position, to get long on the second trade I would have to buy two contracts, one to close the short position and one to initiate a long position.

Figure 4.17 is the same as Figure 4.12, so you can see it without paging back and forth. Why didn't I mark every jig and jag on the entire chart? Because we must leave room for error. You can't catch every up and down move in any market.

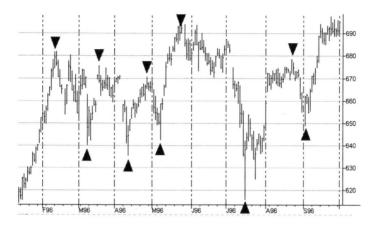

Figure 4.17 S&P 500

Keep in mind that to bring some sense of reality to our calculations, I'm estimating I'll only catch 40 percent of the ideal move. Thus, if a move is small and I miss 30 percent of it on the entry and another 30 percent on the exit, then it'll probably be a losing trade.

Next I must analyze the ideal trades I've marked to see how much the annual wage would be from this effort. Will it be worth my time to trade this instrument?

I start our analysis on a single contract basis. Later on I will look at methods for trading multiple contracts and compounding your winnings.

Looking at each trade, beginning with the first "sell" and closing out at the end of the chart, the hypothetical transaction log would look like (Figure 4.18).

Here's where you take a look at how the "buy and hold" strategy compares to the trading strategy.

Translating the ideal trades into a performance table I get Figure 4.19. That's making some huge assumptions (like we can catch tops and bottoms), but it is a place to start.

Summarizing, a buy and hold strategy where I bought at the ideal low and held until the ideal high would have yielded $45,000, while the ideal trading scenario would have yielded $170,000. Now let's "get real."

Step 3—Accounting for Reality

Now that you've considered the ideal, you've got to get back to reality and take a look at what's more likely to happen.

In PHW analysis I make the assumption that it's possible to capture 40 percent of the ideal profit. So, 40 percent * $170,000 = $68,000, which means you could have made $68,000 that year—a return on investment of 76 percent on your double margin investment of $90,000. Still great! Now all you have to do is create a system that will perform this well. (Much easier said than done.)

Lots of people think they can get into trading and hit the jackpot—get rich overnight. Wrong! Trading is a business, like any other. It takes lots of hard work and time to become an "overnight success."

If today you started a retail business, any business, how long would it take to break even? A fair estimate is three years. And

Approx. Date	Action	Approx. Entry
2/7/96	SELL	680
3/6/96	BUY	645
3/18/96	SELL	670
4/10/96	BUY	640
4/25/96	SELL	670
5/8/96	BUY	650
5/25/96	SELL	690
7/15/96	BUY	630
8/25/96	SELL	670
9/2/96	BUY	650
10/1/96	CLOSE	690

Figure 4.18   Hypothetical Transaction Log

Entry Date	Action	Entry	Exit Date	Exit	Profit/Loss
2/7/96	SELL	680	3/6/96	645	$17,500
3/6/96	BUY	645	3/18/96	670	$12,500
3/18/96	SELL	670	4/10/96	640	$15,000
4/10/96	BUY	640	4/25/96	670	$15,000
4/25/96	SELL	670	5/8/96	650	$10,000
5/8/96	BUY	650	5/25/96	690	$20,000
5/25/96	SELL	690	7/15/96	630	$30,000
7/15/96	BUY	630	8/25/96	670	$20,000
8/25/96	SELL	670	9/2/96	650	$10,000
9/2/96	BUY	650	10/1/96	690	$20,000
				TOTAL	$170,000

Figure 4.19 Performance Table

how much profit would you expect this business to make every year after that? Probably about 10 percent. Those two numbers are industry standards. So, when it takes three years to break-even trading and you make anything over 10 percent per year, you're doing well! That's why I say that 76 percent in the above example is great.

As a further refinement of this step in your research, you could, and in fact should, investigate other time frames. Maybe a 60 minute chart of the S&P would show us shorter-term trades that happen intraday and potentially generate a greater income. If that turns out to be the case, then investigate 30-minute charts as well. Compare several different time frames to see not only which one yields the most profit but also which one is comfortable for you. As they always say in math classes: "That exercise is left to the reader."

5 BRAINSTORMING A NEW SYSTEM

Introduction

After calculating your PHW, the level of profit you could probably achieve, you have an idea where to aim. Knowing how much profit is possible, you have a realistic goal, instead of pie-in-the-sky wishful thinking.

It is very important that you go through this PHW calculation first, before doing anything else in your research. Even if you think it is simplistic or just busywork, do it! It will save you a lot of time and effort in the long run.

The next step in your analysis is to create or borrow an indicator or indicators that will approximate the ideal entries and exits you marked during PHW analysis. All of your idealistic hypothesizing is just so much folly if you can't find a corresponding mathematical model.

Chalkboards and Whiteboards

Brainstorming anything requires an open mind and a meditative state. If you have preconceived notions about the way the market "should" work, throw them aside for now.

Americans tend to look for answers. Both when we negotiate and when we brainstorm, we look for answers. The Japanese have a much longer-term view of the world than we do, thinking beyond each single generation. When they brainstorm, they look for *questions*. The answers will come in time, once you understand the questions.

I find the Japanese method far more productive. When you brainstorm, try the Japanese approach. A properly defined question will generate its own answers.

Stand at a whiteboard (or chalkboard) and write as many questions (hypotheses) as you can think of, without prejudging any of the possible outcomes. Prejudging limits your creativity. Prejudging also is a form of rejection. No one, not even your subconscious, likes to be rejected.

If you are working with a group, one person writes the ideas on the board as individuals within the group call them out. If you are working by yourself, you might want to keep a notebook for your brainstorming ideas, rather than write them on a whiteboard. Each of your premises will become an avenue of investigation, something you can pursue at length later.

When brainstorming you need to make all possible ideas okay without filtering toward the final rules or parameters. Ideas will stimulate more ideas. The flow of open energy will give your neurology permission to come up with a wide variety of questions. You must think of all possibilities as opportunities toward the final outcome.

Explore as many combinations as you can imagine within the limits of your resources and financial practicality. When it comes to brainstorming systems, don't forget that you don't have to do it alone. There are hundreds of books written which have systems or beginnings of systems in them. There are also many systems for sale. Many new traders begin by purchasing an inexpensive system and reverse-engineering. That is, they observe the system in action and see what conclusions they can draw from the system's behavior. Then they apply their newly acquired insights to design their own system.

If you're interested in reading a few books that have system design ideas in them, here is a good starting place:

1. *PPS Trading System* by Curtis M. Arnold
2. *The Dow Jones-Irwin Guide to Trading Systems* by Bruce Babcock, Jr.
3. *Short Term Futures Trading* by Jake Bernstein
4. *The New Technical Trader* by Tushar S. Chande and Stanley Kroll
5. *Street Smarts* by Laurence A. Connors and Linda Bradford Raschke
6. *The Trading Systems ToolKit* by Joe Krutsinger
7. *The Definitive Guide to Futures Trading* by Larry Williams

The Holy Grail is not in any of these books (or any others). By reading these you will get some ideas about where to start and hopefully they will get your creative juices flowing so your brainstorming is more productive.

Reading articles in magazines like mine (*Traders' Catalog & Resource Guide*), *Futures,* and *Technical Analysis of Stocks and Commodities* is another good way to begin your creative process. Often the work of another person will stimulate you to pursue new avenues of exploration. Sometimes the other person's work is enough in itself.

Brainstorming is the creative part of system design. For me, it is the most fun part of the entire process. It is also the most challenging part, as you can work every aspect of your intellect, if you want to.

Overlays

One way to determine what type of indicator might work on our previously marked, ideal PHW chart, is to try them all one at a time. Of course, this would be cumbersome and boring.

Another way to view indicators would be to use your technical analysis software to put every indicator on top of each other on a single chart. This one is overkill, as you'll have a mess you can't read, like the chart in Figure 5.1.

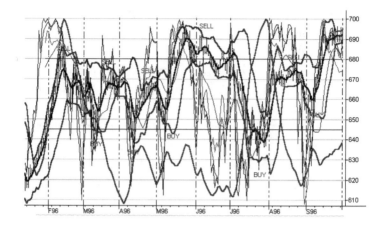

Figure 5.1 Indicators Overlayed on One Chart

But if you pretend for the moment that you are an animator creating a motion picture and create a transparent overlay for each indicator, you can flip through them and begin to learn how each different indicator addresses the condition of the market.

How do you create overlays? Buy transparency film at the office supply store and use it instead of paper in your printer.

You can also tell in this exercise which indicators are telling you the same thing, and which ones would enhance each other. In the beginning of my learning process I went through a lot of overhead transparencies, printing the various markets and various indicators and sitting for hours flipping through them.

What Is True?

Another way to look at market action is through patterns and statistics. Maybe you are not comfortable with the indicators found in most of the technical analysis software packages. Maybe you don't have or don't want a computer. Or, maybe you prefer to work with daily data after the market closes and believe there is some predictive value in pattern recognition.

Patterns in the market are presented in words, based on the five pieces of information you can find in the *Wall Street Journal* or *Investor's Business Daily:* open, high, low, close, and volume. Pattern recognition involves a process of asking yourself repeatedly: "What is true of this data?" If I give you a number sequence like 1,2,3,4, you can observe that data and probably tell me what number comes next. If I give you the sequence 1,1,2,3,5 you might be harder pressed to observe the data and recognize the pattern.

To discover patterns in the market, you can begin in one of three ways:

- Write down each thing that you observe to be true of the current day's data as compared to yesterday's data.
- Write down each thing that you observe to be true of yesterday's data as compared to today's data.
- Read several books by Larry Williams (such as *The Definitive Guide to Futures Trading, Volumes 1 and 2*) and make use of the thousands of patterns he has already discovered and published.

Patterns are presented like this:

- Open of today is higher than close of yesterday, or
- You have had three consecutive down closes

and are analyzed statistically to measure their probability of success and repetition.

In *The Definitive Guide to Futures Trading—Volume 2,* Larry Williams presents patterns thus:

If we have 3 consecutive down closes in the S&P, you have a 64.6% probability of an up day tomorrow.

If yesterday closes up and today's open gaps higher, we will close above yesterday's close about 60% of the time. If we open down we will close below yesterday's close about 70% of the time.

Personally, I find looking at a chart with a moving average on it easier than attempting to recognize patterns. It is a matter of personal preference, though, with one process being a digital approach and the other being continuous.

Looks Like a Duck, Walks Like a Duck

There should be no pride of ownership syndrome evident in your market analysis. You don't have to be Welles Wilder* and invent new and proprietary indicators. Your goal, don't forget, is to make money. Do you really care whether you do it with some brilliant new technique you can name after yourself, or whether you do it with something simple like moving averages? You shouldn't.

The more elegant solution to any problem is always the simplest solution. Simple solutions tend to work over time. Complicated solutions tend to fail as new data creates new and unforeseen situations. Be careful not to fit your answers too closely to the data under observation.

Always follow the market, because the reality is you can't lead it. The market is always right and will do whatever it wants to, independent of your predictions. Dancing backward with your eyes closed is the best way to respond to the markets. To that end, moving averages are great—they follow the trend and slowly change as market conditions change. In my own work I use some pretty fancy moving averages which change themselves dynamically and which are based on exponential moving averages. I like this area of concentration because the exponential averages react quickly to changes in the market and still smooth out erratic market swings.

For now, and for the simplicity of this exercise, we'll take a look at simple moving averages. Keep in mind that a chart is a chart—everything we're doing applies equally well to charts of futures, stocks, mutual funds, and so forth—but for clarity we're going to stick to the chart of the S&P that we used earlier.

*Well-known author and originator of the ADX indicator.

Figure 5.2   S&P 500 with Ideal Entries Marked

As a refresher, Figure 5.2 repeats the chart of the S&P created earlier in our PHW analysis, only this time I've replaced the triangles with the words "buy" and "sell," for the sake of clarity. The software I use can automatically place up and down arrows on the chart where trading signals take place, and when you look at output from that program later, I don't want you to become confused.

The first thing I do is add a moving average to the chart and see how closely it fits the triangles I've used to mark the ideal entries and exits. Since you often hear the 50-period and 20-period moving averages mentioned on television, let's start with those.

Compare the chart on the left in Figure 5.3, showing a 20-period ("shorter") moving average, to the 50-period ("longer") moving average on the right. Notice that when you shorten the length of the MAV (the input value) that the curve more closely approximates the data. Examine both curves to see whether they call out our ideal buys and sells. Clearly the 50-period MAV is too long. It doesn't call out anything, but the 20-period MAV is beginning to show turns near our marks.

Let's go further. This time I'll look at even shorter MAVs; I've cut the "period" (length of the MAV) in half and then in half again, just as a convenient way of guestimating.

63

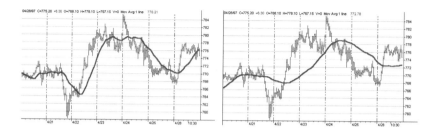

Figure 5.3   S&P 500 20-Period MAV and 50-Period MAV

The 10-period MAV at the left of Figure 5.4 moves nicely with the data, but the 5-period MAV is much closer, isn't it? Does that mean that it is too close? Is the 5-period MAV too "curve-fit" for our use? It depends on how you use it in combination with the MAV you put with it to generate crossovers. Only testing will tell.

I've taken a look at moving averages on the chart, giving us a feel for whether they will fit our purpose, and giving us an initial jumping-off point for the values which might be useful. One way to use the moving average would be to take trades whenever the data crosses the moving average. Looking at the shorter MAVs in Figure 5.4, you can see that this approach would result in an enormous number of whipsaws, since the data is continually crossing back and forth over the MAV. With the 50-period MAV this approach might be feasible, but you would not be able to use it as a reversal system, since you would always be giving back your profits.

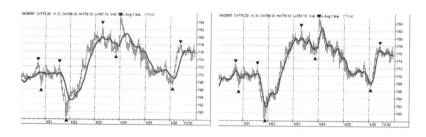

Figure 5.4   10-period MAV and 5-period MAV

The tactic I like with MAVs is to use one short average and one longer average and use the crossover of the two to generate buy and sell signals. With a two moving average system, we look for the places one moving average crosses over the other. When the shorter moving average crosses the longer one we take the trade in the direction of the movement.

Probably the best publicly known system, from my viewpoint, is MACD, developed by Gerald Appel (see Appendix F). MACD stands for Moving Average Convergence-Divergence and was presented in a little 20-page pamphlet in 1985, although it was first developed and introduced in 1979. In that pamphlet Appel states:

> *The Moving Average Convergence-Divergence Trading Method makes use of two moving averages, in this case exponential averages, one faster than the other. In addition, MACDTM employs a signal line, which is a 9-day exponential average of the difference between the two moving averages.*

Because MACD is really looking at the crossover of two moving averages, and because it is available in all the popular technical analysis software, I will use it for the remainder of this exercise as I hone in on a system which approximates the ideal PHW calculations.

Figure 5.5 shows the MACD with its default parameters of 12, 26, and 9 as a starting point for our analysis. The third parameter, 9, is the 9-day exponential average of the difference between the 12-day and 26-day moving averages. This number will remain constant throughout the analysis, so I'm going to drop it from this conversation for now. When I refer to MACD (12, 26) just assume that the third parameter is 9.

Notice how closely the curves of the MACD approximate our ideal signals. True, the signals are a bit late, and in some cases the MACD gives signals where you don't want any. But, it is not a bad start.

In order to approach your ideal trades, you will have to do some experimenting with the input values to the MACD. If you

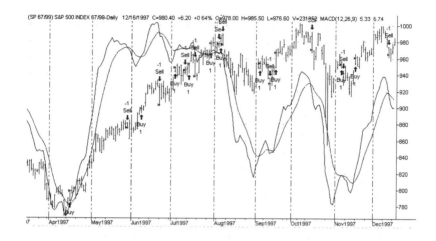

Figure 5.5   MACD with 12, 26, 9 as Input

are doing these calculations by hand, this part of the process will be time consuming and tedious. On the other end of the spectrum, if you have software that allows for optimizing the input values, this part of the experiment can be accomplished within minutes by supplying a range of input values and letting the software do the work.

Using just such an optimizing approach, the software I use suggests use of the value 5 for the shorter MAV and 16 for the longer MAV. In Figure 5.6 you can quickly see that these values not only pinpoint all of your ideal trades, but give lots of extra trades that you don't want.

Here's where the fun begins. As you search for indicators or patterns that will call out your ideal trades, you get to play with mixing and matching indicators. Since you now know that you would like to eliminate the whipsaw areas and the extraneous trades, you can try several options and see what works. Off the top of my head, I'd say you could try:

- Increasing the length of the longer moving average
- Filtering the signals through another indicator

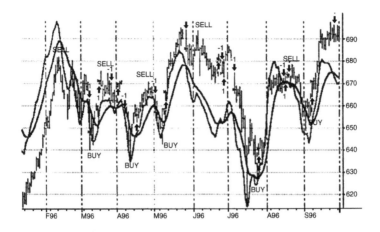

Figure 5.6   MACD with 5, 16, 9 as Input

As you begin to test your theories in the following chapter, you will try both of these suggestions. You will begin to generate reports of each trial in your experiment and to refine the experiment as you learn from each trial.

When you reach the point where your experimental results are consistently close to the theoretical results you postulated at the onset, you've probably got a duck. By the time you have proven your system with empirical methods, you will know that it looks like a duck, that it walks like a duck, and you will accept that it *is a duck* unless proven otherwise.

6 BUILDING A DATABASE

Introduction

Your ability to accurately test your ideas and rely on your results is directly affected by the accuracy of your data. Garbage in—garbage out!

Any time you conduct tests with data that does not exactly represent real market conditions, you are fooling yourself.

Why would you use bad data? Because it's less costly and often easier to use.

Don't ever forget that you get what you pay for. If you skimp on your data, you've jeopardized everything else you'll be doing with regard to designing, testing, and trading your system.

Another case in which people use "bad" data is by purchasing or acquiring continuous contracts. Folks trading stocks, which have long, unbroken histories, don't need to worry about contract expirations, but futures traders face testing their theories over 3-month segments of data. The temptation is to circumvent the tedium of broken data by using continuous data, which has been mathematically "tweaked" to create one long data file. The problem with continuous data is that no trades actually took place at the prices constructed by tweaking.

Joining data from a contract that expires with the contract that becomes active immediately afterward forms continuous data.

For instance, let's say you want to form a continuous contract from the SPM7 and the SPU7 contracts. On expiry date, the closing price of the SPM7 was 898.65 while the closing price of the SPU7 that day was 907.50. To join the contracts seamlessly one must multiply all prices in the SPM7 contract by 1.0098 so that no artificial gap is formed at expiration day. While that leaves the SPU7 contract intact, it creates new data from the SPM7 contract—prices that never happened in real life.

You might want to begin your testing on continuous contract data for ease and speed. As you narrow your research to a firm theory, however, you will need to do your final testing on separate contracts.

In the case of stock trading, whenever a split occurs a similar procedure must be followed to keep the data from having an artificial gap. For instance, if XYZ stock is trading at 100 on June 15 and after the close that day splits 2:1, then the next day it will open at 50. You didn't experience a 50-point loss, however, so you must back-adjust all your data to compensate for the split.

For me, the only way to have confidence in my historical tests is to isolate each contract and run the full set of tests on each individual contract separately. It is a tedious and time-consuming process—and there is currently no single software product that automates this problem correctly. This means that you will end up doing it manually, using spreadsheets to join your results and cull out the meaningless "dirty heads" and "dirty tails."

Data Sources

There are many companies that collect, process, and distribute stock market data. Some of them provide real-time data, some only daily data, and others provide only historical data. Data is delivered in disk, CD-ROM, tape, on-line, satellite, cable, and FM formats. Of course, each company sets its own price schedules, and prices range from nearly free to quite expensive. There are sources of data on the Internet as well, some of them for fee, some free.

Presented in Figure 6.1 is a partial list of data vendors. For a full and regularly updated list of data vendors, you can subscribe to *TC&RG* (*Traders' Catalog & Resource Guide*) by contacting our offices, or you can purchase a single issue through your local bookstore.

How Much Is Enough?

How many tests do you have to run to guarantee that your system works? A better question is, how many trades does it take for the results to be statistically valid?

ADP Financial Information Services	1-800-237-6683
Bloomberg Financial Markets	1-212-318-2000
Bonneville Market Information (BMI)	1-800-255-7374
Bridge Information Systems	1-314-567-8100
Cisco	1-800-800-7227
Commodity Systems, Inc (CSI)	1-800-274-4727
Data Broadcasting (DBC)	1-800-367-4670
Data Transmission Network—DTN	1-800-485-4000 x3330
Dial Data/Division of Track Data Corp.	1-800-275-5544
FutureSource Inc	1-800-621-2628
Genesis Financial Data Service	1-800-808-3282
Knight-Ridder Financial	1-800-537-9617
Morningstar, Inc	1-800-876-5005
PC Quote, Inc.	1-800-225-5657
Prophet Information Services Inc.	1-800-772-8040
Real Time Quotes Inc.	1-800-888-7166
Reuters America Inc	1-800-435-0101
Stock Data Corp	1-410-280-5533
Telerate Systems, Inc	1-201-938-4000
Tick Data, Inc	1-800-822-8425

Figure 6.1 *Commercial Data Vendors*

Let me say first that there are no guarantees! The one thing you can rely on in life is that change happens. Nothing can guarantee you that you will make money in the markets. The markets are always changing. Yet, if you create a system that is not too closely fitted to past market circumstances you can gain some statistical assurance that you have a higher probability of making a profit than losing your shirt.

You will often hear in this industry that 30 trades are sufficient to believe in your system. Balderdash! Thirty trades are a beginning. How much practice would you like your eye surgeon to have before cutting on your eyes? Is thirty enough? Personally I prefer to see something closer to 100 trades before I begin to feel comfortable.

On the other hand, you don't want to go out and buy gigabytes of market data that you may not need. What if you're just beginning and you don't even know yet what you want to trade? Do you buy data for options, stocks, futures? And how much?

My recommendation to you is to begin your analysis with a small sample of several types of data and get a feel for it. Look at charts of many differing time frames. Look at charts of different trading vehicles. Study the movement. In short order you will begin to form a preference.

Take a look at Appendix B where I've listed exchanges, contract sizes, and minimum margin requirements. The margin requirements will, to a large extent, govern the vehicles you trade. If you have $10,000 with which to open your account, you won't be trading the S&P 500. Begin to eliminate items from the list based on your account size. Next, eliminate more items based on their liquidity. *Technical Analysis of Stocks and Commodities* magazine publishes a table each month that ranks the liquidity of futures contracts. (See Figure 6.2.)

Don't buy something you can't sell. You don't want to be the only person trading commodity "x" when it goes limit against you. If the stock or commodity you trade has adequate liquidity you'll usually be able to find someone to take the other side of

Trading Liquidity: Futures

Commodity Futures	Exchange	% Margin	Effective % Margin	Contracts to Trade for Equal Dollar Profit	Relative Contract Liquidity
S & P 500	CME	4.5	7.5	1	
U.S. Treasury Bonds	CBT	2.2	9.8	8	
Eurodollar	IMM	0.2	12.4	52	
Japanese Yen	IMM	2.5	3.1	3	
10 Yr. Treasury Notes	CBT	1.2	8.9	14	
Crude Oil	NYM	10.8	11.9	17	
Corn	CBT	4.4	3.5	14	
Natural Gas	NYM	12.3	9.7	8	
German Mark	IMM	1.7	5.2	9	
Heating Oil #2	NYM	12.6	12.5	13	
Wheat - Soft Red	CBT	4.8	2.9	9	
Gold	NYM	4.7	10.3	16	
Swiss Franc	IMM	1.9	5.5	7	
5 Yr. Treasury Notes	CBT	0.9	15.8	36	
Soybeans	CBT	4.4	9.4	15	
Sugar - World #11	CSCE	6.5	6.2	24	
Cotton #2	CTN	2.7	4.8	10	
Soybean Meal	CBT	6.1	6.7	15	
Coffee C	CSCE	9.2	7.9	4	
Gasoline Unleaded	NYM	10.4	15.2	16	
Mexican Peso	IMM	3.5	6.4	7	
Municipal Bond Index	CBT	1.3	3.7	5	
Copper	NYM	8.6	9.2	12	
Wheat - Hard Red	KC	4.2	3.6	12	
Canadian Dollar	IMM	1.0	9.2	29	
Russell 2000 Index	CME	4.0	8.4	2	
NYSE Composite Index	CTN	1.8	3.1	1	
British Pound	IMM	1.4	15.7	24	
NASDAQ 100 Index	CME	4.5	7.1	3	
Silver	NYM	9.5	46.0	40	
2 Yr. Treasury Notes	CBT	0.4	8.2	22	
Cattle - Live	CME	2.3	12.4	44	
Goldman Sachs Index	CME	3.9	7.0	10	
Soybean Oil	CBT	4.4	30.7	97	
Cocoa	CSCE	4.3	14.9	45	
Libor 1 mo	IMM	0.0	2.5	27	
S & P 500 Mini	CME	4.6	19.5	17	
Dow Jones Ind. Avg. Index	CBOT	4.3	20.5	11	
Wheat - Dark Northern	MPLS	3.7	4.6	15	
Hogs	CME	5.8	13.1	26	
Orange Juice	CTN	6.4	19.8	42	
Canola (Rapeseed U.S. $)	WPG	3.0	7.7	105	
Cattle - Feeder	CME	2.8	7.2	17	
Lumber	CME	2.7	4.1	7	
Oats	CBT	6.0	5.1	27	

CBT — Chicago Board of Trade
CME — Chicago Mercantile Exchange
CSCE — Coffee, Sugar & Cocoa Exchange, New York
CTN — New York Cotton Exchange
IMM — International Monetary Market at CME, Chicago
KC — Kansas City Board of Trade
MCE — MidAmerica Commodity Exchange, Chicago
MPLS — Minneapolis Grain Exchange
NYFE — New York Futures Exchange
NYM — New York Mercantile Exchange
WPG — Winnipeg Commodity Exchange

Margin source: REFCO, Inc.

9808

Figure 6.2 Liquidity Rankings from *Technical Analysis of Stocks and Commodities*

your trade. So, read *Technical Analysis of Stocks and Commodities* first.

Synthetic Contracts

For my initial testing of the S&P 500, I created what I call a synthetic contract. Rather than investigate a complex trading strategy on one contract at a time only to find that it fails, I prefer to do a rough estimate first.

For this purpose I joined together, in continuous contract style, all the front-month contracts, so that each expires and the next takes over on the second Thursday of each quarter. No actual trading ever took place at these prices. But, for my first rough cut I have one long string of data which behaves approximately like the S&P 500.

When testing analog theories like moving averages and oscillators the synthetic contract works great. For testing patterns, it is not so great. Pattern recognition theories often depend on exact prices or exact placement of prices, so if this interests you, use the actual data.

7 SOFTWARE FOR SYSTEMS TESTING

Introduction

You don't need software to test your system ideas. You also don't need a calculator to add up a column of 100 numbers. It just makes it easier.

The great Joe Granville (see Appendix F) doesn't use a computer. He and his wife sit at the table each morning with *Investor's Business Daily* and determine the sums of up-volume and down-volume. They then calculate their proprietary indicators and the analysis follows from there. Joe has been keeping these numbers by hand for over 30 years.

The debonair Mr. Kennedy Gammage (see Appendix F) does not use a computer to keep track of the McClellan Oscillator and Summation Index. Neither do the McClellans themselves.

There's something to be said for keeping your numbers and charts manually. You certainly get a better "feel" for the data. The drawback, of course, is in the difficulty of trying a large variety of ideas if you do all the calculating by hand.

Having acknowledged those dedicated few who steadfastly maintain charts and data by hand, I'll move on to the more likely scenario: using computers to analyze your data.

For the most part, you needn't spend a fortune on your trading computer. Optimally, you only need a computer which will accomplish the tasks of trading, and which you can dedicate to the process. Having a second computer with all the bells and whistles keeps all other tasks off your trading computer. A Windows 95 capable PC with a moderate amount of memory and a moderate hard drive will run most trading software. A CD-ROM is a plus, since most software and data these days comes on CD. If you download end-of-day data from your data vendor or from the Internet, you will want to have a modem on the computer. You can get this configuration for about $1,000 either mail-order or at your local computer store. Check with the software vendor before determining your final configuration, as some of the more recent have much higher memory and hard disk space requirements.

Purchasing a monitor is a matter of personal preference. You can acquire a used color monitor for as little as $80 or spend as much as $4,000 on the latest large format flat screens.

In the beginning of my trading career I ran MasterChartist, a Roberts-Slade product, and had my Macintosh driving four 21″ color monitors. At the time I thought I would need that much power to see everything that was going on in the markets. I kept 16 charts open on each monitor and scanned them all day long. I was exhausted by the end of each trading day. Experience taught me that I couldn't process that much information, and that it wasn't furthering my main goal—making money. Now I trade with one small 14″ color monitor and let the software do all the work, alerting me to special situations and bringing up the corresponding chart.

In short, you probably don't need to spend more than $2,000 on your total hardware setup.

Software, like any other product, gets cheaper as the market for it gets larger. Competition is a good thing. A product's price is also determined by its utility. Specialty products with specific application are more expensive than broad-use, generalized consumer products. Don't expect to pay $29.95 for trading software. If you are serious about trading, you will spend several thousand dollars on software.

Furthermore, since all traders are capitalists (they are, aren't they?) and looking to make a profit, they won't begrudge other capitalists their profit. If you want good software with a good maintenance and development team behind it, be willing to pay for it. This is not one of the places to try to save money.

What's Available and What Does It Do?

It is not my intent to list all of the trading software for you in this book. I publish another book (*Traders' Catalog & Resource Guide*) which is comprehensive in nature and updated quarterly, where you can browse vendors and products to your heart's content. In *Trading 102* I'll discuss just a few of the software products that do the job well. Mentioning a product herein does not imply an endorsement of the product, nor does a product's absence from this book imply any lack of confidence therein.

Software is a matter of personal preference. The software I use may not be right for you. The only way you will know which products you are most comfortable with is to use them.

Of course, you don't want to purchase each and every one, just to settle on the one final product you want to use. So, how can you use them if you don't buy them? Request demos. All of the leading software vendors have demo disks that they are happy to send you. With demos in hand, you can play around with each product and compare their utility, ease-of-use, and fitness for your purpose. For your convenience, if you'd like to find all the demos in one place, come to *The Money Mentor* (http://www.moneymentor.com) where you can download them from the Internet for free and at your leisure. Then you can do your comparison shopping in private.

The software I'll cover in this chapter includes:

- Programming Languages (like C++ or Basic)
- Excalibur
- TradeStation

- MetaStock
- Window On WallStreet
- SuperCharts
- TickerWatcher

At the end of each product section, I give you the code for a simple moving average crossover system, so you can get a feel for the language they use. Again, which language you are more comfortable with will be a matter or personal preference.

Write It Yourself with C++ or Basic

Your best bet for having full control of your outcome is to do it yourself. Any software product you purchase will do part of what you want it to and will not do part of what you want it to. No software does everything. Nor would you want it to attempt to do so, as bells and whistles slow the software down.

The disadvantages of doing it yourself are that programming is time consuming, and it is costly. A standalone program to effectively trade the markets would take about three person-years to code and test. At $125 per hour, 2000 hours per year, the project would cost you approximately $750,000. Clearly it's less expensive to purchase a $2,000 product that does most of what you want.

Nevertheless, if you are so inclined, and don't already know C++ or VisualBasic (the two languages currently in common use), your local college or trade school will have classes. Barring that avenue, check the Internet. There you will find online classes and videotapes for sale. Both The Learning Tree, at http://www .learningtree.com and LearnKey at http://www.learnkey.com have a broad collection of training CDs and videos to assist you.

Excalibur

Probably the most versatile and most powerful program for designing and testing trading systems, Excalibur is not only a C++ program, but it is also open architecture, so that you can use it as an engine and include your own C++ programs into it.

Versatility in using Excalibur means you can accomplish virtually anything you want to, but that the major amount of the three person-years of programming is already done.

Excalibur Macro Language is the simple front-end language used for defining rules and indicators in Excalibur. C coding of system rules and indicators is optional. With Excalibur you can test multiple systems in a portfolio and view the cumulative equity results; most data formats are acceptable; historical tests and optimization, as well as multiple commodity tests, are no problem.

The folks at Futures Truth make and market Excalibur and can be contacted at:

John Hill
Futures Truth
Hendersonville, NC
1-704-697-0273

Futures Truth's charter is to test and rate trading systems, and they use Excalibur to do so.

Excalibur Code for Dual Moving Average Crossover

```
MOVAVG1=SMAVG (CLOSE(D1), L1)
MOVAVG2=SMAVG (CLOSE(D1), L2)
IF (MOVAVG1.GT.MOVAVG2) THEN
    PRICE=OPEN (D)
    FILTER='CROSS BUY'
    GO TO 500
    ENDIF
IF (MOVAVG1.LT.MOVAVG2) THEN
    PRICE=OPEN(D)
    FILTER='CROSS SELL'
    GO TO 600
    ENDIF
```

TradeStation

In 1989, when I started designing and testing computerized trading systems, Omega Research made the only program which could assist in the backtesting process. Their SystemWriter software, a DOS program, ran on my 286 computer for days at a time, as it processed the thousands of tests I designed.

Within a few years Omega Research had taken the System-Writer concept a leap further, creating their TradeStation product.

TradeStation runs under Windows 95, will test real-time as well as daily data, and includes its own programming environment, which they call EasyLanguage.

As TradeStation grows and improves, it is also requiring larger computers to run it. The upcoming version 5.0 (which I am now beta-testing) purports to require a 200mb Pentium with at least 32mb of memory.

TradeStation's bells and whistles include historical testing, automatic notification of impending trades, pager or e-mail notification, and a wealth of indicators and built-in systems.

If you are interested in this product, feel free to contact

Kevin Feuerlicht or Ralph Cruz
Omega Research
Miami, FL
1-800-422-8587 or 1-800-292-3453

When you tell the folks at Omega Research that Sunny sent you, they usually throw in their historical data CD-Rom or sometimes even the EasyLanguage training videos.

TradeStation Code for Dual Moving Average Crossover

```
If Average (C,L1) > Average (C,L2) Then Buy
on Close;
If Average (C,L1) < Average (C,L2) Then Sell
on Close;
```

MetaStock

Probably the most stable and mature product of the group, Meta-Stock is a product of Equis International, a Reuters company. MetaStock sports the highest quality graphics of the products mentioned in this chapter, approaching publication quality.

MetaStock is the only trading software that currently claims Microsoft Office compatibility. As such, MetaStock conforms to the look and feel of all your other Microsoft software, which makes it intuitive and easy to use. One of MetaStock's nicest features is that you can drag and drop just about everything. If you want to move an indicator, just click on it and drag away. If you want to change the characteristics of something, right click the mouse. They've gone a long way toward making this program a very handy tool, not a stumbling block. MetaStock is so intuitive, there's not much to learn.

MetaStock's historical testing is fast and efficient. Testing and optimizing a system with MetaStock is virtually as simple as pressing the key combination CTRL+T. (See Figure 7.1.)

MetaStock Code for Dual Moving Average Crossover

```
Enter Long:
Cross (Mov(C,opt1,S), Mov(C,opt2,S))
Enter Short:
Cross(Mov(C,opt2,S), Mov(C,opt1,S))
```

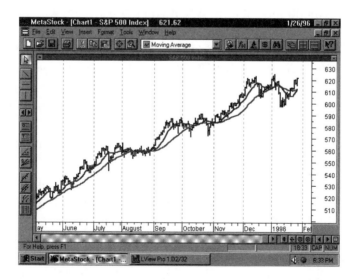

Figure 7.1 Typical MetaStock Chart

81

To learn more about MetaStock and Equis International, contact them at:

Mike Denison or Dan Smith
Equis International, Inc.
3950 South 700 East, Ste 100
Salt Lake City, UT 84107
1-800-882-3040

Window On WallStreet

Formerly Windows On WallStreet, the popular trading software made by the Window On WallStreet (WOW) folks is called Day Trader. The name of the software does not preclude holding positions overnight. Nor does it mean you can only trade daily bars. Day Trader is a full-featured, powerful, real-time program that is powerful enough for the professional and easy enough for the novice.

Historical systems testing with Day Trader is of a different flavor (at least at this writing) than was observed in the other products mentioned herein. When you test a system with this software, there is no optimization feature that lets you try every moving average from 1 to 20, for instance. You must try them one at a time. (I'm trying to talk WOW into changing this very soon.) However, they have included a unique feature that lets you test and rank multiple systems at once. With this handy tool you can test a CCI, Moving Average, Stochastics, MACD (or anything else your heart desires) with the click of one button, ranking their performance in comparison to each other.

In addition to allowing a message to be sent to your pager on alert conditions, Day Trader provides a number of default alert sounds that you can hear from the next room.

Much like MetaStock, Day Trader is as easy to use as clicking your mouse. Click an arrow, click a color, and the chart changes. One soothing feature of Day Trader is the flexibility in color choice. I am particularly fond of the light yellow background I can put on all my charts.

Changing from tick data to 15-minute bars to daily bars is as simple as using a pull-down menu. The most popular 15 choices are included in the list, followed by an option for you to define your own time period. Day Trader has a few more exciting features worth mentioning here. (See Figure 7.2.)

WOW's SmartScan feature enables one to scan an entire list of symbols for technical and fundamental conditions, as well as for any new signals. Automated reports can be generated while you sleep, so that you are ready for the day when you get up the next morning.

I could go on and on about this new addition to our repertoire of trading software, but let's stop with this feature: online research. WOW has provided a link for dialing any online service you wish, at the click of a button. See a stock you like and want to know more? Just get online.

Day Trader Code for Dual Moving Average Crossover

```
Enter Long:
(mov(c,Period1,s)>mov(c,Period2,s))
Enter Short:
(mov(c,Period1,s)<mov(c,Period2,s))
```

Figure 7.2 Typical Day Trader Chart

To learn more about Day Trader and Window On WallStreet, contact them at:

Stephanie Cherry or David Barnes
Window On WallStreet
1820 N Glenville Dr Ste 100
Richardson, TX 75081
1-800-998-8439

SuperCharts

As you will see from the code below, SuperCharts is an offshoot of TradeStation. Originally developed for serious systems testers, TradeStation is just too serious for the average trader. Omega's SuperCharts program is priced for the consumer and easy to use. Essentially a pared down version of their professional product, SuperCharts and MetaStock are frequently seen as competitive products.

SuperCharts Code for Dual Moving Average Crossover

```
Long Entry:
Average (Close,Length1) crosses over
Average (Close,Length2)
Short Entry:
Average (Close,Length1) crosses below
Average (Close,Length2)
```

If you are interested in SuperCharts, feel free to contact

Kevin Feuerlicht or Ralph Cruz
Omega Research
Miami, FL
1-800-422-8587 or 1-800-292-3453

8 DESIGNING YOUR SYSTEM

Introduction

In the previous chapters you began the process of brainstorming your system. Don't mistake the beginning for the end, however. You still are not even close to where you need to be to trade. Before beginning to paper trade you must:

- Refine and specify the system you brainstormed
- Test the system thoroughly
- Prove the cardinal profitability constructs
- Determine optimal stops
- Apply money management techniques

Profits Swept Under

If you are one of those "woulda, coulda, shoulda" people, get over it. You will always miss some of the best trades. You will always leave money on the table. Consider it a job well done if you can pick up 40–50 percent of the tradable moves in the market.

Don't kick yourself when a trade has gone bad; figure out what you can learn from it. Write your lesson down. Read it again and again. Learn from your mistakes and consider them valuable education.

Think about the overall outcome of your trading. Don't focus on any one individual trade. Remember to manage your profits and view this as a long-term job. You are not a gambler, you are a business person.

Design of Experiments

In biology or chemistry lab you pose a question (your hypothesis) and run various tests to prove or disprove your hypothesis. That is exactly what I do with system design for trading.

Further, in biology or chemistry lab you make certain you have a sterile environment so as not to contaminate your outcome, and you allow only one variable to change at a time, holding all other parameters constant. Every experiment must be exactly the same and under the same conditions, except for the variable. If you change even one thing, you must go back and re-perform each experiment with the same new conditions.

Putting Your Ideas on Paper

You've done your brainstorming. Now you must commit your ideas to paper.

Remember the exercise from Chapter 3, where we talked about building a peanut butter and jelly sandwich? As you begin to specify the rules that govern your trading decisions, keep this exercise in mind. Everything that you establish algorithmically must be clear and concise.

For instance,

sometimes I look for the moving average to cross and sometimes I look for a breakout

is not precise. What does "sometimes" mean? What are the exact conditions?

In designing and defining your system you must specify every instruction clearly, so a monkey can trade it for you. Let's get a little more specific about "sometimes." If you said:

*when the market is moving fast I look for a breakout and
when the market is moving slowly I look for the moving
average to cross*

you would be getting more specific. However, you're not there
yet. What does "fast" mean? What does "slowly" mean?

These terms must be defined so that there will be no ambiguity for the monkey. You could say that the market is moving fast
when the absolute value of the momentum indicator is greater
than one. That would be precise. A condition like this can be
expressed mathematically, and thus we can test it with a computer. Such a condition might look like

```
ABS (MOM(C,10))>1.0
```

That's the sort of specific rule I want you to create. If you are having trouble with this part of your trading, give me a call. I'm at
760-930-1050 in Carlsbad, CA.

Accepting the Results

There are several standards by which you will want to judge your
system. Does it meet your personal goals? How does it compare
to other traders? How does it compare to the stock market itself?
How does it compare to widely accepted standards of excellence?

It is a good idea to have all of these standards of comparison
in writing, in the front of your research log notebook. That way,
when you've reached a goal, you will know it. Otherwise, you are
likely to continually raise the standard and never find acceptable
results. This is rather like setting stops in the market when you
enter the trade. That way you don't change your mind when the
going gets tough.

Setting Your Personal Goals

In setting your personal goals you will ask yourself some very
serious questions. Do you want to be a full-time trader? Do you

want to be an investor, and keep your "day job"? If you want to be a full-time trader, with no other source of income, what is the minimum monthly dollar figure on which you can survive?

What are your musts and what are your wants? What would you settle for? What would your neurology be comfortable with? On the other side of that coin, what would you absolutely not accept?

Make a checklist for yourself. Prioritize your musts and wants. Keep in mind that not all months will be winners. Trading is the one business that sometimes pays you and sometimes you pay it.

Comparing Yourself to Other Traders

Don't compare your trading performance to that of your buddies or members of your local trading club. Chances are they will not tell you the truth about their overall performance anyway.

By comparing your results with that of other traders, I mean for you to look for published performance records to use in comparison.

Futures (see Appendix F) magazine runs a monthly review of managed money. Presented in tabular form, *Futures* gives you the most recently available information on the market as a whole and on the trading performance of CTAs and public funds. For instance, in the January 1997 issue of *Futures,* they reported October 1996 performance of the S&P to be +2.76 percent, while the average CTA returned +5.53 percent. Performance varies from month to month, so I like to keep a spreadsheet log of this report in order to get a longer term view.

MAR (see Appendix F) (Managed Account Reports) compiles a quarterly report of trading advisor's performance. This report costs several hundred dollars and is several hundred pages thick. From MAR's *Quarterly Performance Report* you can gather in-depth information about each individual advisor, as well as taking a look at the overall performance of the industry.

Again many hundreds of pages, *The Stark Report,* published by International Traders Research (see Appendix F) and *The Bar-*

clay Institutional Report, published by Barclay Trading Group, Ltd., (see Appendix F) both offer an enormous amount of information about individual trading advisors.

Another source, possibly closer to home, of statistics on how well other traders perform is *Futures Truth.* A bimonthly report published by John Hill of Futures Truth, (see Appendix F) this report is more manageable both from price and number of pages standpoints, and it covers trading systems' performance. Hill's group independently tests and trades publicly available trading systems and reports their performance. Averaging all the results together would be a good way for you to compare your system's performance to other systems.

When you make comparisons, keep in mind that more factors play a role in performance than just the bottom line. You can't expect to be a master bridge player or a black diamond skier on the first try. It takes years of experience and practice—and a lot of falls. Consider, when rating yourself against others, the length of time your competition has been in business, their education, the type of trading they engage in, and the amount of risk they are willing to take. Take into account the instrument or combination of instruments they are trading. For instance, a stock trader usually makes a lower annual return than a stock index futures trader. A mutual fund trader might make more than a stock trader. And some options traders make a higher return than some futures traders.

Just as most magazines pick only the most perfect models to pose for their photographs, a trader will often only tell you about the best trades. The real world doesn't look like that. Be sure you have all the facts before you choose a measuring stick.

The indices published monthly in *Futures* are easily accessible and inexpensive to track. Keeping a running chart of these indices and your monthly return allows you to monitor your performance on a comparative, monthly basis.

In Figures 8.2 and 8.5, later in this chapter, we present charts of several standards of performance, overlaid to facilitate comparison.

The Average Professional Trader

If you can do as well at your new business as the average professional trader, you will be exceptional. These people are pros. They have been at it for years and usually have access to all the latest and greatest tools and research.

What does the average professional trader make? If you take a look at another Internet site, you can find several databases of Commodity Trading Advisors (CTAs) and their performance, from which you can estimate what to expect of yourselves.

At *The Money Mentor* (http://www.moneymentor.com) look for Commodity Trading Advisors, Advisory Services, or Market Advisory. Under these listings you will find references to the services which rate trading advisors. From International Traders Research, Inc. you will find reports and rankings, showing the performance of the 435 CTAs they track. Their top 40 CTAs for the most recent 12-month period range in Return on Account from 482 percent down to 40 percent. I don't know about you, but that makes me feel like I should be making 300 or 400 percent per year.

Let's step back just a bit and look at the broader picture. Rather than look up the performance of each CTA individually and divide by 435, I called International Traders Research, Inc., in La Jolla, California (619-459-0818) and asked them what the average CTA's annual return is. They kindly responded with the following:

In the attached table you'll see that only CTAs with at least 36 months' trading history are included. This is our ITR Index, and is the only way to run this sample. For example, in March of '95, there were 365 CTAs with at least a 36-month track record. We then calculate the average ROR [Rate of Return] (NOT dollar weighted) of all the CTAs in the sample, for all the months, and from that a regular cumulative VAMI ROR for the year.

In case you are wondering what ROR and VAMI are, take a look at the formulas in Chapter 11, System Performance Assessment.

We can learn quite a lot from studying the information in Figure 8.1. First, of course, the obvious. For 1995 the average CTA had 21.82 percent return on his account; for 1996 the average CTA had 14.56 percent return on his account. If we average these two years, we get an average return of 18.19 percent. Okay, that's only two years, not nearly enough information from which to

DATE	AVG ROR	TOT P/L	TOT EQTY	TOT # CTAS	VAMI	ANNUAL ROR
Jan-95	−0.0103	$−219,846	$13,189,596	365	990	
Feb-95	0.0376	$428,608	$13,514,537	365	1,027	
Mar-95	0.0731	$915,582	$14,253,651	364	1,102	
Apr-95	0.0137	$232,838	$14,486,963	364	1,117	
May-95	0.0181	$149,353	$14,820,359	364	1,137	
Jun-95	−0.0118	$−223,902	$13,991,779	364	1,124	
Jul-95	−0.0089	$−220,015	$13,879,264	364	1,114	
Aug-95	0.0295	$174,424	$14,175,723	365	1,147	
Sep-95	0.0053	$−137,916	$13,971,958	362	1,153	
Oct-95	−0.0013	$6,183	$13,699,619	356	1,151	
Nov-95	0.0167	$213,807	$13,815,911	356	1,171	
Dec-95	0.0407	$493,230	$13,794,243	354	1,218	21.82%
Jan-96	0.0308	$383,113	$14,176,704	347	1,031	
Feb-96	−0.0379	$−667,621	$13,137,615	343	992	
Mar-96	0.0152	$129,556	$13,119,473	340	1,007	
Apr-96	0.0559	$540,195	$13,786,507	332	1,063	
May-96	−0.0091	$−223,937	$13,423,505	332	1,053	
Jun-96	0.0016	$84,329	$13,494,752	326	1,055	
Jul-96	−0.0202	$−204,757	$13,367,614	317	1,034	
Aug-96	−0.0073	$20,573	$13,495,731	314	1,026	
Sep-96	0.0316	$425,390	$13,010,428	307	1,059	
Oct-96	0.0546	$857,326	$13,858,639	294	1,116	
Nov-96	0.0398	$811,634	$15,647,500	288	1,161	
Dec-96	−0.0132	$−241,647	$15,126,748	284	1,146	14.56%

Source: International Traders Research, Inc.

Figure 8.1 Commodity Trading Advisors

draw major conclusions. But, for our purposes in this exercise, it's sufficient. We just want to know if we can keep up.

So if you are averaging 18 percent per year, or more, in those two years you are doing better than the average professional trader.

Now let's take a look at what other facts you can glean from this table. My eye first goes to the Total Profit/Loss column, seeing that in both 1995 and 1996 the pros had four losing months. Moreover, it seems that when they have a loss, they don't immediately recover. Since a chart is worth a thousand numbers, let's put the VAMI from this table in graphical form (Figure 8.2) and look at the extent of the drawdown for both years.

In 1995 the VAMI hit a peak in May, and it took until August to recover. In 1996 the pros hit a peak in April, and it took until September to recover. This is typical of trading. Think about it and make contingency arrangements in your business plan. The profit line doesn't just go straight up. What would you do in a year where you didn't bring in any trading profits for five months?

Comparing Yourself to the Stock Market

It is very difficult to consistently perform better than the overall stock market. Yet, the performance of a broad indicator like the

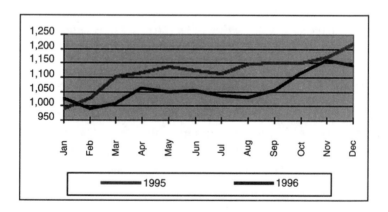

Figure 8.2 VAMI Chart of Average CTA Performance

S&P 500 or the Value Line or the NASDAQ is a good measure of your success. If you can consistently keep your line above the stock market's line on the chart, you're doing great!

So, how do you keep track of these measuring sticks? Pick an index and keep a log of it. At the end of each month you will log the closing price of the index (let's use the S&P 500 Index) into your spreadsheet and compute the percentage return for that month. In another column, log your own performance and compute the percentage return for the month. (See Figure 8.3.)

Okay, now what? You have a spreadsheet log, but what does it mean? In order to compare apples to apples you must start both your own performance and the performance of the index from the same value. Comparing your $20,000 to the S&P Index value of 758.15 doesn't mean much.

Professional traders use VAMI to compare their results to each other and to other indices.

Definition:

VAMI—Value Added Monthly Index
Represents the growth of $1,000 invested at the start of the track record based on the historical monthly rates of return.

Date	S&P	S&P ROR	Your System	Your ROR
12/31/96	758.15		$20,000	
1/31/97	802.85	5.90%	$21,000	5.00%
2/28/97	805.65	0.35%	$23,345	11.17%
3/31/97	764.00	−5.17%	$22,845	−2.14%
4/30/97	810.80	6.13%	$28,344	24.07%
5/30/97	859.30	5.98%	$29,344	3.53%
6/30/97	890.25	3.60%	$26,844	−8.52%
7/31/97	957.95	7.60%	$29,199	8.77%
8/29/97	903.20	−5.72%	$30,199	3.42%

Figure 8.3 Your Performance Comparison Log (Hypothetical)

$$VAMI_{i+1} = VAMI_i * (1 + ROR)$$

where ROR is the monthly percentage rate of return.

In order for us to do this, we need to add two columns to the spreadsheet: "S&P VAMI" and "Your VAMI." We will use $1,000 as the initial value of each column and use the preceding formula to compute subsequent values. See Figure 8.4.

Since we all know that a picture is worth a thousand words, let's take a look at these numbers graphically, in Figure 8.5.

A mere glance at this chart tells you that your (albeit hypothetical) system has outperformed the S&P.

Standards of Excellence

There are a few measures of success that are inarguably mandatory to having a profitable system. There are many other statistics which indicate the robustness of your system or its inherent risk, but those values are matters of personal preference.

In the family of mandatory measures, a positive mathematical expectation is paramount. I'm sure you will agree that if your system is mathematically expected to lose money, it is not one to be

Date	S&P	S&P ROR	Your System	Your ROR	S&P VAMI	Your VAMI
12/31/96	758.15		$20,000		1,000	1,000
1/31/97	802.85	5.90%	$21,000	5.00%	1,059	1,050
2/28/97	805.65	0.35%	$23,345	11.17%	1,063	1,167
3/31/97	764.00	−5.17%	$22,845	−2.14%	1,008	1,142
4/30/97	810.80	6.13%	$28,344	24.07%	1,069	1,417
5/30/97	859.30	5.98%	$29,344	3.53%	1,133	1,467
6/30/97	890.25	3.60%	$26,844	−8.52%	1,174	1,342
7/31/97	957.95	7.60%	$29,199	8.77%	1,264	1,460
8/29/97	903.20	−5.72%	$30,199	3.42%	1,191	1,510

Figure 8.4 Your Performance Comparison Log with VAMI (Hypothetical)

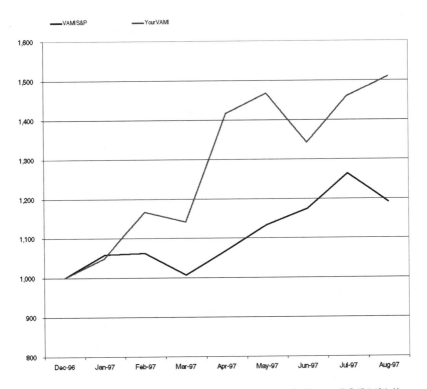

Figure 8.5 Comparative Chart of Your VAMI vs. S&P VAMI

traded. Beyond that, I would look for a system which is not only positive, but also one that will generate enough profit to pay for the fees associated with trading it.

The next standard you should look at is the size of winning trades compared to losing trades and how often you win. Ideally, you would like to have your wins be substantially larger than your losses and to win more often than you lose. But how often and how big? There is no single answer to that question, since in part it is colored by personal preference and willingness to assume risk. In fact, the answer is derived by a bit of fuzzy logic. (Fuzzy logic is easily understood by using the words "roughly" or "loosely." For instance, your wins should be "roughly" twice the size of your losses.)

95

All traders grapple with these concepts, as you can see from this message I received by e-mail from John Bollinger (see Appendix F):

There are really only two ways to improve your investment performance; you can either increase the number of winning trades versus losing trades, or you can increase the size of your winners versus your losers. Our research suggests that the combination of a ratio of about two winning trades for every losing trade and winning trades that are twice as big as losing trades is the standard of excellence. Think of it as a barrier that separates the truly successful from the merely successful. Of course there are lots of combinations along the frontier that will give you the same results. More winners versus losers, but a smaller winning margin; or less winners versus losers and a much larger margin. As with all critical variables in investing, these are soft, fuzzy if you will. What is important is to be in the general area of success, not at a specific ratio.

In the next chapter I will explore these standards at length through definitions of Cardinal Profitability Constructs™ (CPC).

9 FORMULAE FOR SYSTEMS DEVELOPMENT

The Proof Is in the Pudding

As a mathematician, the word "proven" means something very precise to me. Let's first get the definition of that single word out of the way, so we'll have an agreement about its meaning. Webster's defines it as "tested by experiment" or "established as true." While this is part of what I mean by the word "proven," I also mean that we must have a measure or measures of success which quantify "true." And further, we need a specific set of procedures that constitute the "experiment."

Thus, to have a proven system that you can have confidence in year after year, you must establish its validity by experimentation. And, its validity is measured by a set of numbers that we trust will produce winning results over the long term.

Once you have a proven system, you would do well to trade it mechanically. That is, you should follow its instructions without hesitation or second-guessing.

Mechanical trading is very similar to flying by instruments in an airplane. First you test your instruments, and then you test them again, THEN you must rely on those instruments and follow your flight plan without regard to the fog around you. If you override your instruments, you just might fly into a mountain. The same is true with mechanical trading. Establish your system, test it, test it again, and then trust your tests. Trading then becomes as easy as 1, 2, 3.

Getting from Here to There

Okay, you have calculated your PHW, you have brainstormed your system ideas, you have run a vast number of tests and kept detailed logs. Now what?

Your system seems pretty good. But, how do you know? How can you quantify its robustness? How can you tell whether it will withstand the test of time and changing conditions?

You have a pretty good handle on that issue by dividing your data into thirds and back- and forward-testing. You showed that it still performs on different sets of data. Now, how can you quantify that in some other way?

Cardinal Profitability Constructs (CPC)

When evaluating an idea, or theory, for its long-term potential, I like to have a quantitative measure of the theory. With a quantitative measure I can compare systems to each other. In a sense, I can give each system a score.

Here's what I look at:

1. Mathematical expectation (ME)
2. Percent profitability (P)
3. Ratio of the average profitable trade to the average losing trade (P/L ratio)
4. Profit factor (PF)
5. Return on account (ROA)

I call these my Cardinal Profitability Constructs (CPC).

If a system I have designed passes muster through this rigorous set of CPC conditions, after already passing through the first set of tests, I'm ready to trade it.*

The qualifying conditions I look for in the CPC numbers are these:

- Mathematical expectation > 0.0
- Percent profitability ≥ 35 percent
- (P/L ratio) × (Profit factor) ≥ 3.0
- Return on account ≥ 20 percent

All well and good, you say, but where do I get those numbers? Okay, hang on just a little bit here, I'm going to do some mathematics. Nothing strenuous, though, so don't stop reading.

Often the statistics you need to form the CPCs are included in the standard reports of your technical analysis software. Even so, you should be able to calculate them yourself and understand the underlying concepts.

ME: Mathematical Expectation

Mathematical expectation tells you whether you should expect to win or lose in the long run. Calculate mathematical expectation using this formula:

$$ME = [(1 + A) * P] - 1, \text{ where}$$

$$P = \text{Probability of winning and}$$

$$A = (\text{Amount you can win})/(\text{Amount you can lose}).$$

Ralph Vince, in *Portfolio Management Formulas* demonstrates that you'll never end up a winner with a trading system that has a mathematical expectation less than zero. He goes on to

---

*Please note that I am not saying that this level of CPC numbers will guarantee success. I am suggesting that this is a vigorous test and one I use in my own system evaluation.

say that any system with an ME greater than zero can be improved through money management techniques, while no money management scheme will make a system with ME < 0 a winner.

That's why you calculate this value first. There's no use calculating further if you find that your new system fails this first test.

Let's take a look at the individual components of the equation for mathematical expectation.

P: Probability of Winning or Percent Profitability

This one's simple. If you have 100 trades total in your database, and of those, 40 are winners, then you figure the percent profitability thus:

P = [number of profitable trades]/[total number of trades]

So, P = 40/100 = 40 percent. It's how many times we expect to be profitable out of the total number of trades.

A: (Amount You Can Win)/(Amount You Can Lose) or Ratio of the Average Profitable Trade to the Average Losing Trade

Sometimes referred to as the profit to loss ratio, for this calculation you simply divide the average winner by the average loser. Thus, where

AW = the dollar value of the average winning trade
(the average of all your wins),

AL = the dollar value of the average losing trade
(the average of all your losses),

then

A = AW/AL

A few examples will illustrate just how this equation applies.

Example 1: Given an even probability of winning and losing (P = 0.5) and average win and average loss of equal magnitude (AW = 1, AL = 1), what is the mathematical expectation (ME)?

$$ME = [(1 + A) * P] - 1$$

$$ME = [(1 + 1/1) * 0.5] - 1$$

$$ME = [(2) * 0.5] - 1$$

$$ME = [1] - 1$$

$$ME = 0$$

In this example, we are looking at the breakeven situation. Here you're just as likely to win as to lose and you win the same amount as you lose.

Example 2: Let's look at one of the situations often seen advertised. Great claims are made of a system that sports 80 percent wins. You're ecstatic. This looks like a safe bet; a system you want to trade right away. Right?

Not necessarily. The ad hasn't told you the value for A. What is the magnitude of the average win? What about the average loss? What happens if the average win is $200 and the average loss is $800 in an 80 percent winning system?

$$ME = [(1 + AW/AL) * P] - 1$$

$$ME = [(1 + 200/800) * 0.8] - 1$$

$$ME = [(1000/800) * 0.8] - 1$$

$$ME = [1] - 1$$

$$ME = 0$$

Another breakeven trading system! Good thing you don't believe everything you see in advertising.

Example 3: Now you're skeptical. If 50-50 can fail you, and 80-20 can fail you, how do you find a winning system?

Many, many professional traders use systems that sustain 35–45 percent accuracy. Isn't that terribly risky? Not necessarily; it depends on two things: your emotional makeup and the size of A (average win/average loss).

A 35 percent accurate system means that 35 percent of the trades are winning trades. But, from a psychological standpoint, it means that 65 percent of the trades are losers! Only *you* can say whether you are disciplined enough to continue following a system that loses most of the time.

Regarding the parameters you can determine objectively, let's compute A for a system which is 35 percent accurate and where the average win is $500 and the average loss is $200.

$$ME = [(1 + AW/AL) * P] - 1$$

$$ME = [(1 + 500/200) * 0.35] - 1$$

$$ME = [(700/200) * 0.35] - 1$$

$$ME = [3.5 * .35] - 1$$

$$ME = 0.225$$

How about that? At first glance you would probably turn down the 35 percent accurate system. But, of the three examples you've looked at, this is the only one with a positive mathematical expectation.

The relationship between P, the percentage of time you have winning trades, and the size of your average trade governs your mathematical expectation. After the section covering profit factor, we'll take a look at a table that illustrates this relationship.

Expected Reward

What does having a positive ME tell you? A system with a +ME is likely to make money over the long term. Can you lose money on a system that has a +ME? Sure. You can also flip a coin 100 times and have the first 50 flips turn up heads. It's not likely, but it's possible. And, in fact, it is an outcome that must be considered in your modeling.

In all likelihood, if you have the capital base to withstand losses, and you don't risk too much of it at once, following a system with a +ME will eventually lead to profits.

How can you estimate *how much profit* the system is likely to generate? In *Money Management Strategies for Futures Traders,* Nauzer J. Balsara (see Appendix F) gives a formula for expected reward (ER), which I translate thus:

$$ER = (PW * AW) - (PL * AL)$$

where

$$ER = \text{expected reward}$$

$$PW = \text{probability of winning}$$

$$AW = \text{average win}$$

$$PL = \text{probability of losing}$$

$$AL = \text{average loss}$$

Assume you've conducted your historical testing and find that over the test period you have 100 trades, of which 35 are winners and 65 are losers. You know that the average winning trade yields $500 and the average losing trade costs us $200. (You'll recognize this as the information from Example 3 above.)

Using Balsara's formula:

$$ER = (35/100) * (\$500) - (65/100) * (\$200)$$

$$ER = (\$175) - (\$130)$$

$$ER = \$45$$

Thus, statistically you can expect $45 net profit per trade. With 100 trades you can expect to net $4,500.

There are many combinations of CPC numbers that result in an overall winning system, as John Bollinger so aptly stated at the end of the previous chapter. The key to picking a set that works for you lies in your discipline level. How likely are you to continue trading a system that loses more often than it wins?

The CPC numbers are interrelated on a sliding scale, which is represented in Figure 9.1. Any system with ME > 0 is theoretically a winning system. For this exercise, let's say we are looking for an ME = 0.2. This value for ME is achieved through any combination listed in Figure 9.1.

Further, since A is the quotient of two numbers, it can be formed from many different sets of numbers. Figure 9.2 displays some of the possible combinations.

What you see from the figures is that as P (your probability of winning) gets smaller the size of your average win must continue to get larger proportional to your average loss. In an 80 percent accurate system you can have an AW of $200 and an AL of $1000 and still come out a winner. However, in a 35 percent accurate system, you must have AW nearly 2.5 times as large as AL to end up in the same place.

Let me give you a clue here, lest you spend the rest of your life looking for an 80 percent system. Professional traders usually

$$ME = [(1 + A) * P] - 1$$

ME	A = AW/AL	P
.2	0.20	100%
.2	0.50	80%
.2	1.00	60%
.2	1.40	50%
.2	2.00	40%
.2	2.43	35%
.2	3.00	30%

Figure 9.1   ME Value

A	AW	AL
.2	$200	$1,000
.2	$300	$1,500
.2	$400	$2,000
.5	$200	$400
.5	$300	$600
.5	$400	$800
1.0	$200	$200
1.0	$300	$300
1.0	$400	$400
1.4	$200	$142
1.4	$300	$214
1.4	$400	$285
2.0	$200	$100
2.0	$300	$150
2.0	$400	$200
2.43	$200	$82
2.43	$300	$123
2.43	$400	$165
3.0	$200	$67
3.0	$300	$100
3.0	$400	$133

Figure 9.2   Amount You Can Win/Amount You Can Lose

trade systems with accuracy between 30 percent and 45 percent, while looking for large wins and small losses.

In *Maximum Adverse Excursion,** John Sweeney (Editor of *Technical Analysis of Stocks and Commodities* magazine) examines the relationships among winning trades, losing trades, and their adverse excursions—the amount a trade goes into losing territory. In the process he creates a list of trades, both win-

Maximum Adverse Excursion, John Sweeney, 1997, John Wiley & Sons, Inc.

ners and losers, and directs your attention to the maximum adverse excursion (MAE). Key to you is his statement about trading systems:

The anomalous characteristic of the list is that there are more winners than losers, something I've rarely found in trading systems.

So, John Sweeney is also telling you that most trading systems have more losers than winners!

PF: Profit Factor

The profit factor tells us how robust the system is by comparing the gross profit to the gross loss. It tells us how many dollars the trading system made for every dollar it lost. Thus,

$$PF = Gross\ Profit/Gross\ Loss$$

A profit factor of one (1.0) means you're making and losing the same amount of money, that is, breakeven. If the profit factor is less than 1.0 you're making less money than you're losing, that is, this is not a winning system.

Return on Account

Your ROA number will vary, depending on how much capital it took to handle the drawdowns of your system. The more money you put into the account, with the same dollars net profit, the lower this percentage will be. For purposes of testing, I let the computer determine the account size required and calculate the ROA on that. Clearly you want the ROA to be a positive number, and hopefully a large positive number. Even if it is now a huge number, however, you can eventually increase the total return using money management techniques, as long as you have a positive mathematical expectation.

More Measures of Success

Professional traders and money managers have standard measures of success they use to compare their trading to each other and to define the reliability of their systems. Books like Barclay's *Institutional Report, Managed Account Reports,* and *Stark Report* provide these statistics for each trader they follow.

Sharpe Ratio

Probably the most well-known and widely followed of these measures is the *Sharpe Ratio.* This ratio, developed by Professor William R. Sharpe of Stanford University, compares the rate of reward from an investment with the risk incurred in gaining that reward. The formula is annualized geometric rate of return minus rate of return on a risk-free investment divided by the annualized arithmetic standard deviation. Or,

$$\text{Sharpe Ratio} = (ROR - RFI)/STDEV$$

where

      ROR = your system's rate of return

      RFI = the risk free rate of return (usually T-Bills)

      $STDEV$ = the standard deviation of your system's return

If you are interested in pursuing this line of investigation further, *Managed Futures* by Carl C. Peters goes into great depth on the subject of performance evaluation.

Consistency and Predictability

It is important to know that your likelihood of success is evenly spread over the months and years of your performance, and not a pattern of many months of losses followed by a single large gain.

If your system is consistent, then it will produce roughly the same rate of return month after month, or year after year.

Consistent performance will usually fall into the normal distribution pattern, with a peak in the middle and tails at either end. Figure 9.3 shows one way to look at the consistency of your performance. The numbers for this chart are fictitious, just so you can grasp the concept. Plug in the numbers for your own performance, hypothetical or actual, and you will get a visual idea of how consistent your system is. If the chart appears random, and not a normal distribution, you will spend your trading career in a state of constant surprise. To be able to plan and budget, you will want to see most of your performance results appear in a cluster pattern like the one in Figure 9.3.

Predictability or projectability compares your current performance to your past performance, measuring what percent of the time you come close to repeating your historical average return, within some small error factor. Let's say that your average return for the last three years was 25 percent per year. If you use an error factor of 5 percent, then any return greater than 20 percent during the next year will count as a successful forecast. If the year following that you make 10 percent, then at that point your system

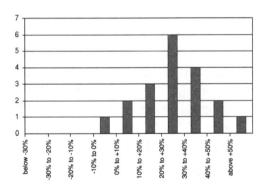

Figure 9.3 Distribution of Returns

has predictability of 50 percent. Clearly, the object here is to maximize this number. As I flipped through the MAR Report, the average projectability of professional traders seemed to be around 50 percent.

Recovery Time

Related to the consistency of your system, a key measure of your success is the amount of time it takes for you to recover from drawdown. When your system encounters a losing streak, how long does it take for you to get back on your feet again? Drawdown is measured from peak to valley on your equity curve. Recovery is measured from valley to the first place you are once again in new profit territory.

Looking at the equity of the S&P 500 itself, in Figure 9.4, note the two periods of drawdown (circled). The first valley ends in the fourth month and has recovered by the fifth month. Thus, the "months to recovery" (MTR) for the first drawdown is 1.0. The second period of drawdown is a bit deeper, starting in the middle of the fifth month and ending in the middle of the sixth month. We are not fully recovered from the damage until the eighth month, so the MTR for this drawdown is 2.0. The average MTR then, for this nine-month chart, is 1.5.

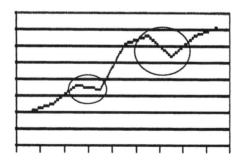

Figure 9.4   Months to Recovery

Average of Worst Drawdowns

If your worst drawdown is 25 percent, but it only occurs once in the 10-year history of your trading, and the rest of the time your drawdowns are around 10 percent, that is an important distinction.

This measure of your system's risk allows you to do "worst case" analysis and also "most likely case" analysis. You will make your decisions differently if your worst case happens only once in a lifetime, as opposed to regularly.

To determine your system's average of worst drawdowns, first calculate all the drawdowns in your system's history. Then calculate the average of the worst five. This number is more meaningful than maximum drawdown by itself.

Conclusion

Clearly, anyone can develop a trading system; but not all trading systems are created equal. Before you consider trading real dollars on anything, make sure that you've at least analyzed and met or exceeded the above criteria. Having done so, then you can begin to focus your efforts on improving your system through proper placement of stops, dynamically adjusting indicators, and money management techniques.

10 BACKTESTING AND OPTIMIZING YOUR SYSTEM

Introduction

Every system has certain constants. These constants can always be turned into variables and then optimized. The danger is that most systems crated on past data get over-optimized, curve-fitted to that past data, so that in hindsight the results look terrific. Yet in the real world tomorrow's optimal parameters are almost always not the same as yesterday's optimal parameters. The system that worked so well on past data falls apart in the real world.

Optimization is not the enemy—abuse of optimization is.
—Ralph Vince, *Portfolio Management Formulas*

Ours is an industry full of contradictions. The regulating bodies of the futures industry require that commodity trading advisors provide any potential clients with a full listing of all past trading performance. The same regulating body requires that in the performance record the following statement appear:

Past results are not necessarily indicative of future results.

Now I don't know about you, but the way that I interpret that is: "Past results mean nothing." But, if that is true, why do they make you present them? Of course, I'm being facetious, but the point is that we rely on past performance, hoping it will in some way be assurance of our future success. To a large extent, the only way we can make any predictions at all is to test our theories over historical data. Yet, nothing about these tests guarantees that the market will perform tomorrow like it has in the past. That's a pretty scary admonition.

Nevertheless, since it's all we have, we base our research on historical testing and stay alert for changes in the markets that might indicate system failure. We'll discuss system failure later on.

Definition:

Optimization
Finding the best or most favorable conditions or parameters.

In system testing, the most favorable conditions are represented by the largest net profit, usually. There are circumstances under which you would not consider the greatest net profit to be the best system. For instance, you might reject a system which has 1000 trades per month and a huge net profit in favor of a system which trades 30 times per month and makes a large, but not the largest, net profit.

When you optimize the parameters in your system, you look for variables that produce the greatest net profit over the longest period of time.

Definition:

Curve-Fitting
Developing complicated rules that map known conditions.

If you optimize a moving average to loosely fit market conditions from 1982 to 1997, you might do pretty well trading in the future. But if you optimize it so that it very closely fits the market, and you add conditions that match current and past events, you have curve-fitted the data. A curve-fitted system often does not behave well (profitably) into the future.

As you search the universe for the "Holy Grail" you will encounter many, many stumbling blocks along the way. Many of your optimizations will not work; some will. To assist you in sorting the good paths from the not so good, it is best to keep detailed records.

Your Lab Book

With each and every test run you should maintain thorough and complete records of the variables used as input and the outcome of the trial. These logs will be instrumental in narrowing your choices down to the last few crucial experiments.

The more meticulous you are in your record keeping, the more you will benefit from hindsight. For years I have kept 3-ring binders of my research ideas and testing results. I recommend you do the same. Make yourself some forms, either by hand or with your computer. Make copies of the forms, or print out several from your computer, and be consistent. *Use your forms.*

For my lab book I use the same form for every test I do. I keep track of the variables input to the software and of the resulting statistics which show the success or failure of the idea.

You will want to design your own forms, but the following figures show a few of the formats I use. They may help you get an idea of what you want to do for yourself. (See Figure 10.1.)

Your initial log of experiments will look something like Figure 10.2 where you fill in the profit/loss figures as you run each separate test. With this log you will be able to separate the good results from the bad results.

As you get farther along in your testing, you will begin to keep more detailed records in order to distinguish between varying levels of good results. You will begin looking for more information from each test than just the net profit.

113

Date & Time: _____

System Name & Description: _____

Input Values: _____

FASTMA	SLOWMA	MACDMA	Net Profit/Loss
			$
			$
			$
			$
			$
			$

Figure 10.1   Form Format

Date & Time: _____

System Name & Description: _____

Input Values: _____

FASTMA	SLOWMA	MACDMA	Net Profit/Loss
12	26	9	$13,250
11	26	9	$10,250
10	26	9	$ 9,250
12	25	9	$12,500
11	25	9	$10,500
10	25	9	$ 9,000

Figure 10.2   Logging Experiments

There are several analysis and testing products (listed in *Trading 101—How to Trade Like a Pro*) which give various system statistics as the result of each test. One new product has come on the market since writing the first book, which is worth taking a look at. Called Performance Summary Plus (PSP), by RINA Systems (1-513-575-9128), this add-on to TradeStation does an incredible job of evaluating your portfolio. PSP looks at systems analysis, trade analysis, run-up, drawdown, and risk/reward ratios, as well as efficiency analysis, protective stop analysis and lots more.

Some of the useful statistics you might be looking for are:

- Total net profit
- Net profit from long trades
- Net profit from short trades
- Open position profit/loss
- Gross profit
- Gross loss
- Total number of trades
- Percent profitable
- Number of winning trades
- Number of losing trades
- Largest winning trade
- Largest losing trade
- Average winning trade
- Average losing trade
- Ratio average win: average loss
- Average trade (win and loss)
- Maximum consecutive winners
- Maximum consecutive losers
- Average number of bars in winners
- Average number of bars in losers
- Maximum drawdown
- Maximum run-up
- Profit factor
- Return on account

With this much information to sort through, your logs become critically important. How else would you keep track of the subtle difference between test results?

A more advanced form, for keeping additional statistics, might look like Figure 10.3.

Eventually you will need lots of 3-ring binders or file folders to categorize the experiments you've run and their results. Research and testing is not an overnight project. In fact, you should plan this phase of your work as if you were developing a software product to sell at CompUSA. It may take many months as you grind through the tedium of running and logging each experiment. In the end it will be well worth it; you will have done your homework, and you will have the evidence that gives you the confidence to follow the system.

Am I Done Yet?

How much data do you need to use for testing before you can be sure of the replicability of the results? And furthermore, is there a way to keep from curve-fitting the data?

As stated in Chapter 6, I like to see at least 100 trades from a system before I am willing to trade it with real money. Most often

Date & Time:

System Name & Description:

Input Values:

FastMA	SlowM	Net	Long	Short	PF	ROA	DD	#Trd	%Pfbl	BigW	BigL	AvgTr

Figure 10.3   More Advanced Log

you will hear the number 30 tossed around, but I am not personally comfortable with that few examples.

To test a system over a set of data which produces only 30 trades would generate a very nice model that would work well over that specific set of historical data. But as the markets fluctuate and the mood changes from bull, to bear, to sideways and back again, the model with 30 trades would probably prove to be only accurate over that subset of data that you initially developed it for.

Not only do I like to see 100 trades before I believe a system works, I like the data to include up moves, down moves and sideways moves.

Often I am asked what time period the 100 trades should cover. My response is: as much time as it takes to get 100 trades. If your system generates 100 trades per year, you need a year's worth of data. If it generates 100 trades in 10 years, you need 10 year's worth of data.

The key to successful system generation is to start your research using only a portion of the available data. After completing the entire research process for that limited set of data, we would engage in "backtesting" and "forward testing." I divide my data into thirds, testing the middle third first as I generate theories and systems. (See Figure 10.4.)

Using the data from 1987 through 1995 for testing, the data from 1987 through the end of 1989 is historical data to your new system. Thus, any testing you do on data that happened before the period you've proven is "backtesting." Likewise, the data that comes after 1992 (which you didn't even peek at) is future data to the system. In effect, you are running a blind trial that could not have been curve-fitted, because you didn't have the data as part of the initial design.

1987	1988	1989	1990	1991	1992	1993	1994	1995
II			Data Set I			III		

Figure 10.4 Testing Your Data by Thirds

If your system performs reasonably well (within your expectations) over the backward test and the forward test, you just might have a tradable system. But, don't trade it yet, there's more you have to find out.

With the help of today's software, you can do the experiments just a bit faster. While you will end up in a mire of confusion if you vary too many things at once, with state-of-the-art software you can allow more than one variable to change simultaneously.

Let's say you were investigating a simple moving average crossover system and wanted to test every possible combination from 3 to 30. That means you want to test every moving average crossover from (3,3), (3,4), (3,5), (3,6) . . . (3,30), etc. all the way to (30,3), (30,4), (30,5) . . . (30,30).

In TradeStation we would vary the two lengths by specifying a range of values, like Figure 10.5.

Likewise for the second variable, Length 2, you would input 3 for the start value, 30 for the stop value, and 1 for the increment. In shorthand notation this would be expressed as 3:30:1. This combination would cause the software to run 784 tests automatically for us.

In MetaStock, running the same tests requires the same input in a very similar format, as in Figure 10.6.

When the software finishes running the 784 tests, it displays the results in tabular or report format. You will be able to view the net results of all the tests and compare them to the values used for

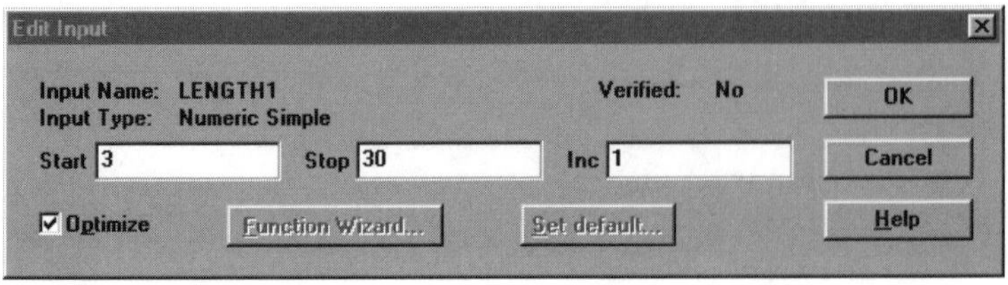

Figure 10.5 TradeStation Optimization Input Screen

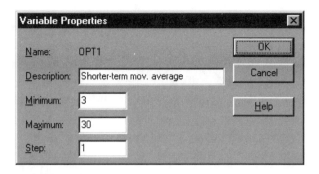

Figure 10.6 MetaStock Optimization Input Screen

	LENGTH1	LENGTH2	NetPrft	L:NetPrft	S:NetPrft	PFact	ROA	MaxDD	#Trds	%Prft
1	3.00	19.00	-9000.00	42350.00	-51350.00	.91	-15.89	56625.00	37	30
2	3.00	6.00	-9700.00	44900.00	-54600.00	.94	-16.52	58700.00	67	33
3	3.00	5.00	3600.00	51550.00	-47950.00	1.02	6.19	58125.00	79	30
4	3.00	4.00	10250.00	44150.00	-54400.00	.95	-23.26	44075.00	125	43
5	3.00	9.00	6950.00	49125.00	-42175.00	1.06	10.21	68050.00	50	38
6	3.00	3.00	.00	.00	.00	100.00	.00	.00	0	0
7	4.00	4.00	.00	.00	.00	100.00	.00	.00	0	0
8	4.00	8.00	-10600.00	43050.00	-53650.00	.92	-22.36	47400.00	57	32
9	4.00	5.00	4850.00	52175.00	-47325.00	1.03	7.28	66600.00	95	35
10	4.00	3.00	10250.00	54400.00	-44150.00	1.05	22.36	45850.00	125	57
11	4.00	7.00	1400.00	49050.00	-47650.00	1.01	2.75	51000.00	61	34
12	4.00	9.00	6250.00	48950.00	-42700.00	1.06	12.56	49750.00	50	32
13	5.00	6.00	-11100.00	42800.00	-53900.00	.93	-29.94	37075.00	87	38
14	5.00	5.00	.00	.00	.00	100.00	.00	.00	0	0
15	5.00	7.00	3550.00	49025.00	-45475.00	1.03	7.43	47800.00	65	37

Optimization Report - SPDAILY-Daily

Figure 10.7 Optimization Report from TradeStation

input. Viewing each parameter that was used as input, and comparing the net profit from each set, allows you to determine the optimal input parameters for your eventual system.

Figures 10.7 and 10.8 show reports generated from two popular technical analysis programs, TradeStation and MetaStock.

Keep in mind that you must run these tests blindly on the middle third of your data, and use the best results from those to test the first and last thirds of the data. Don't overoptimize.

119

Test...	Status	Net Profit	Perce...	Tot...	Win...	Losi...	Avg ...
197	OK	918.3591	91.84	26	11	15	3.2406
225	OK	859.5099	85.95	26	10	16	3.5904
309	OK	842.8533	84.29	22	8	14	4.1565
142	OK	840.5439	84.05	30	12	18	3.2704
141	OK	840.3539	84.04	34	13	21	3.3569
366	OK	824.3519	82.44	21	7	14	4.2782
115	OK	811.8630	81.19	28	10	18	3.8668
422	OK	805.1755	80.52	21	7	14	4.1872
337	OK	802.7518	80.28	21	8	13	3.5081
159	OK	794.3935	79.44	32	12	20	3.2139

Figure 10.8 Optimization Report from MetaStock

Comfort Zones

Having run thousands of tests, how do you make sense of them? You've produced a huge table of numbers, but how does it relate to the system you are trying to find?

For me, the easiest way to interpret the results is to export the optimization results into a spreadsheet where I can rearrange the rows and columns.

Some programs allow you to export the data using a command they have provided called *export* or *save as.* Some programs have no specific provision for this task, and you will have to trick it a bit, by printing the output to a file.

The file you have saved to disk will be in ASCII text format, delimited by commas. Opening the file with your spreadsheet program is then simply a matter of importing the text file. I use Microsoft Excel, so the following illustrations will be from that program. You should be able to do just about the same thing with any spreadsheet.

Figure 10.9 shows the initial view of the imported spreadsheet. Your objective is to see if there is any clustering of parameters that produces a "comfort zone" of good results. If you find that, for instance, dual moving average crossovers of (3,15),

	A	B	C	D	E	F	G	H		I	J	K
1	L1	L2	NetPrft	#Trds	%Prft	#WTrds	#LTrds	AvgWL		AvgTrd	PFact	% ROA
2	3.	13	$ (32,713)	39	31	12	27	1.59	$	(839)	0.71	(59.05)
3	3.	14	$ (1,113)	36	50	18	18.	0.98	$	(31)	0.98	(3.30)
4	3.	15	$ 41,688	32	56	18	14.	1.40	$	1,303	1.80	116.89
5	3.	16	$ 21,825	28	46	13	15	1.65	$	779	1.43	59.09
6	3.	17	$ 34,750	26	50	13	13.	1.86	$	1,337	1.86	176.73
7	3.	18	$ 34,925	26	62	16	10	1.16	$	1,343	1.85	198.44
8	3.	19	$ 40,938	27	63	17	10	1.27	$	1,516	2.16	204.43
9	3.	20	$ 30,188	21	52	11	10	1.63	$	1,438	1.80	101.73
10	3.	21	$ 52,938	19	58	11	8.	2.38	$	2,786	3.27	290.87
11	3.	22	$ 39,188	21	52	11	10	1.88	$	1,866	2.07	144.47
12	3.	23	$ 45,213	19	53	10	9	1.97	$	2,380	2.19	119.37
13	3.	24	$ 47,600	17	53	9	8.	2.05	$	2,800	2.30	147.88
14	3.	25	$ 28,950	19	37	7	12	2.87	$	1,524	1.68	78.75
15	3.	26	$ 10,163	19	26	5	14.	3.37	$	535	1.20	25.39
16	4.	13	$ (12,813)	41	44	18	23.	1.11	$	(313)	0.87	(29.00)
17	4.	14	$ 11,188	38	50	19	19	1.17	$	294	1.17	34.28
18	4.	15	$ 49,050	32	56	18	14.	1.61	$	1,533	2.08	180.91
19	4.	16	$ 55,575	25	56	14	11	2.07	$	2,223	2.64	361.46
20	4.	17	$ 60,825	25	64	16	9	1.65	$	2,433	2.94	339.80
21	4.	18	$ 44,550	23	57	13	10	1.75	$	1,937	2.27	169.39
22	4.	19	$ 62,800	19	63	12	7	1.95	$	3,305	3.34	267.09
23	4.	20	$ 52,513	19	58	11	8.	2.03	$	2,764	2.80	184.25
24	4.	21	$ 50,138	19	58	11	8.	1.89	$	2,639	2.60	169.60
25	4.	22	$ 48,125	19	58	11	8.	1.84	$	2,533	2.53	160.82
26	4.	23	$ 46,175	17	47	8	9	2.71	$	2,716	2.41	161.59
27	4.	24	$ 28,275	17	41	7	10	2.50	$	1,663	1.75	94.17

Figure 10.9 Initial Excel Spreadsheet

(3,16), and (3,17) all produce acceptable net profits, you'll be much more comfortable trading in this range than if you find isolated parameters with no clustering.

The first step to finding clusters is to sort the spreadsheet by net profit. That parameter is in column C of our spreadsheet. Let's set the sort to "descending," so the largest net profit will be on top.

If you are not familiar with these concepts, you have several resources to bring you up to speed on your spreadsheet program. First, the help command in the spreadsheet provides an abundance of information to get you started. Next, you should still have the user's manual for the program. If those two aren't enough, your local community college will probably have classes you can take on a Saturday or in the evening. Further, most bookstores carry video "how to" tapes and "for dummies" books that can start you on your way.

Figure 10.10 shows the result of our sort.

LENGTH1	LENGTH2	NetPrft	L:NetPrft	S:NetPrft	PFact	ROA	MaxDD
12	15	84050	68150	15900	1.37	362.28	−23200
3	21	77650	62250	15400	1.41	284.95	−27250
9	15	76825	61275	15550	1.37	279.87	−27450
3	18	71600	59225	12375	1.35	391.26	−18300
9	21	67700	56175	11525	1.43	250.74	−27000
3	24	65550	56200	9350	1.35	189.73	−34550
12	18	63650	54825	8825	1.36	277.34	−22950
9	18	61725	54175	7550	1.35	293.23	−21050
9	27	60500	53075	7425	1.44	221	−27375
9	24	55625	51700	3925	1.37	185.73	−29950
6	24	52200	48775	3425	1.3	211.12	−24725
18	30	47500	49300	−1800	1.37	142.64	−33300
3	27	44100	44200	−100	1.24	140.33	−31425
27	30	44075	46525	−2450	1.26	127.29	−34625
9	30	44050	45850	−1800	1.31	141.19	−31200
24	30	39700	44000	−4300	1.28	123.48	−32150
6	27	36475	41850	−5375	1.22	142.9	−25525
15	18	35175	41525	−6350	1.16	144.16	−24400
24	27	35075	42100	−7025	1.18	72.62	−48300

Figure 10.10   Spreadsheet Sorted by Descending Net Profit

The entire spreadsheet is not included in this book, as it's too large. But you're only interested in the net profit column right now, and in the most profitable results, so this will be adequate.

The second step is to mark the acceptable results so that we will be able to identify them after re-sorting the spreadsheet by columns A and B. I like using color, in particular light yellow, for this purpose. In Excel there is a tool that looks like a paint bucket, which is used to fill the selected cells with color. I highlight the cells with the best results, down to and including 80 percent of the maximum net profit. Since 80 percent of 84050 is 67240, you'll highlight down to row 6. The result will look like Figure 10.11.

LENGTH1	LENGTH2	NetPrft	L:NetPrft	S:NetPrft
12	15	84050	68150	15900
3	21	77650	62250	15400
9	15	76825	61275	15550
3	18	71600	59225	12375
9	21	67700	56175	11525
3	24	65550	56200	9350
12	18	63650	54825	8825

Figure 10.11   Spreadsheet with Best Net Profits Highlighted

Now when we sort the spreadsheet by columns A and B, which contain the data for Length1 and Length2, the highlighted cells will be easy to spot, as in Figure 10.12.

There will be several clusters highlighted yellow. As you run your tests on more and more data, you will begin to notice cluster areas where there are overlaps in good performance from month to month, quarter to quarter, or from year to year. You will want to concentrate your testing and design efforts in these areas, where the predominance of clustering lies.

LENGTH1	LENGTH2	NetPrft	L:NetPrft	S:NetPrft
3	3	0	0	0
3	6	27775	38800	−11025
3	9	−31350	7800	−39150
3	12	4400	26800	−22400
3	15	24975	36775	−11800
3	18	71600	59225	12375
3	21	77650	62250	15400

Figure 10.12   Spreadsheet Sorted by Length1 and Length2

Branching Off

How do you know when to stop? As your research progresses, you will come up with more and more ideas, each new one leading to several others. Some ideas will work, some won't. Some will seem to work at first, only to fail when you introduce data from the first and last thirds. You will find many dead ends as you wind through this maze.

Don't despair. Photographers take hundreds of pictures to come up with one good one. Only one out of ten new businesses survives. You've got to kiss a lot of frogs before you find the prince. That's the nature of this business. You must generate hundreds of possible paths before finding the few that will actually result in profitable systems.

There is only one way to find your way back out of the maze, however. Keep good notes. If you ultimately want to use your results to trade, you must remember what the results were. Don't let piles of optimization reports and performance summaries accumulate on your desk (or floor). Use the forms you've created and keep them organized in notebooks, with a table of contents or database that gives you an overall view of where you've been and where you are going.

One last thought on tree branches. One pitfall many traders encounter is the "grass is greener" syndrome. There is a propensity to make a career of finding systems, rather than trading the one or two with acceptable results.

Once you find acceptable results, get down to the business of trading. There will always be another system, a better system, a smarter trader. Avoid the temptation to spend your life in pursuit of the Holy Grail.

11 SYSTEM PERFORMANCE ASSESSMENT

Introduction

How much is enough? Are you still on track? Has the system failed? How do you compare to other traders? How do you compare to the instrument itself? How does your actual trading compare to your system's hypothetical trading?

Have you asked yourself these questions? If you haven't, you should! You should know your system inside and out, backwards and forwards. You should be intimately familiar with the statistics that illustrate which ways your system can succeed and which ways it can fail.

Of course, don't forget that nothing ever performs exactly in the future as it did in the past. You can flip a coin 50 times and get 50 heads. But, statistically you should see results similar to those of the model.

This chapter will take a look at some of the ways you can gauge the success or failure of your system, even before you trade it.

Keeping Track

With good bookkeeping you can stay ahead of the game. If you keep close account of your trades, your tests, and your mistakes, you'll be ahead of 90 percent of the traders against whom you are competing.

At the very least you must know whether your trade was a buy or a sell, when the trade was made and what you were trading. Figure 11.1 shows a handy little form I use to keep up-to-date with the essentials:

Actually, I make this form on my computer (using a spreadsheet) and I print out hundreds of them. I then keep these records in a 3-ring binder, as well as enter the information into the spreadsheet in the computer. I find that the double entry method still works best for me. It's easy to get flustered, or not to have the spreadsheet running at the time you place the trade. Then you lose track of whether you are long or short and it's embarrassing to have to ask your broker to tell you.

Measurements

There is no end to the ways you can analyze your success (or failure). You can run statistics from now until doomsday, but the only thing that really matters in the end is whether you are turning a profit. I will go over a few important measurements here, but if you are interested in thoroughly examining your performance, PSP (by Rina Systems) does a thorough job.

Date	Time	Buy Sell Cancel	Qty	Instru.	mmyy	Strike	Ticket	System Fill	Actual Fill
2/19/97	1:00p	Sell	10	SP	H7		277	814.90	814.95

Figure 11.1   Keep Up-to-Date Form

Slippage

The first measure of your success in trading will come from the form (in Figure 11.1) into which you have been conscientiously entering data. Notice that the last two columns are "System Fill" and "Actual Fill." I add another column in my computerized spreadsheet, which is the difference between the last two columns. Your first measurement will be in this "Difference" column. This is what I call slippage.

For example, if my system tells me to buy, I will call the broker and enter the market order right then. Let's say that the price showing on my computer screen at the moment the signal came was 814.90. While I am waiting on the phone for the order to be filled, the ongoing market activity can cause the price to go up, down, or stay the same. The broker comes back on the line and tells me my order was filled at 814.95.

The difference between my desired fill (814.90) and my actual fill (814.95) is 0.05, which amounts to $25 on the S&P. Because the order was to buy, that's $25 loss due to slippage. If the order had been to sell, the subtraction would be performed in the opposite order. It is to my benefit to sell at a high price. In this case, we would have a $25 gain due to slippage.

Usually you will experience both negative and positive slippage. Negative slippage is when your fill is worse than you had hoped, and you incur a loss due to the fill price. Positive slippage occurs when your fill is better than you expected and you end up making more money on the trade than your system expected. Often you will find that positive and negative slippage cancel each other out, especially in fast, liquid markets like the S&P. But, even if they don't, slippage is one of those "cost of doing business" items. You just learn to live with it.

Slippage will vary from broker to broker. The closer you are to the floor, the less slippage you are likely to experience. If your account is set up so that you call your broker, who calls a trading desk, who calls the floor, who signals in the order, you are likely to get a worse fill than someone who calls straight to the floor or even to the trading desk on the floor.

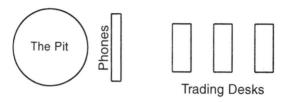

Figure 11.2 Trading Floor Schematic

Figure 11.2 is a rough sketch of the floor, so you can see what I mean.

ROR

ROR just means rate of return. Sometimes you'll see it referred to as ROI (return on investment) and sometimes as ROA (return on account). Whatever you call it, it is all the same stuff: how much money did you make, expressed as a percentage of your initial investment.

For example, if you invested $1,000 and made $200, your rate of return would be $200/1000 = 20/100 = 2/10 = 0.2$. Fractionally, this is said "two tenths." Expressed as a percentage, this is a 20 percent ROR.

VAMI

VAMI is an acronym for value added monthly index. Professional traders compare their performance to each other using this statistic. The reason it is so widely used is that it allows you to compare apples to apples.

If you are trading a $50,000 account and your friend is trading a $1,000,000 account, how can you meaningfully compare your successes and failures?

VAMI represents the growth of $1,000 invested at the start of the track record based on historical monthly rates of return. The formula for its calculation is:

$$VAMI_{i+1} = VAMI_i * (1 + ROR)$$

Thus, you would take the percentage return made on your actual account and apply it to the theoretical $1,000 account. Your friend would be doing the same calculations with his or her account. So, each month you would be able to compare apples to apples.

Figure 11.3 is a spreadsheet illustration of the method.

MAE

MAE stands for maximum adverse excursion. You could also call this "how bad could it get?" Officially, John Sweeney in *Maximum Adverse Excursion* defines it thus:

> **Maximum Adverse Excursion**
> Excursion is just the change in price from our point of entry, measured every bar. When prices move against your trade, that is adversity. From this comes the term adverse excursion. MAE is an acronym for the worst that it gets while in a particular position.

	Beginning	P/L	ROR	Ending	VAMI $1,000
January	$50,000	$1,000	2.0%	$51,000	$1,020
February	$51,000	$2,000	3.9%	$53,000	$1,060
March	$53,000	$1,000	1.9%	$54,000	$1,080
April	$54,000	$(500)	−0.9%	$53,500	$1,070
May	$53,500	$3,000	5.6%	$56,500	$1,130
June	$56,500	$(1,500)	−2.7%	$55,000	$1,100
July	$55,000	$1,200	2.2%	$56,200	$1,124
August	$56,200	$1,500	2.7%	$57,700	$1,154
September	$57,700	$1,800	3.1%	$59,500	$1,190
October	$59,500	$(900)	−1.5%	$58,600	$1,172
November	$58,600	$1,500	2.6%	$60,100	$1,202
December	$60,100	$750	1.2%	$60,850	$1,217
ANNUAL TOTAL		$10,850	21.7%		

Figure 11.3 VAMI Calculation

A chart of MAE would look like the spidery chart in Figure 11.4.

In the 150 or so pages of *Maximum Adverse Excursion,* Sweeney goes into great detail about the use of this powerful tool for reducing your risk. I have found that MAE is particularly useful in positioning stops. One avenue for you to try in your systems design might be to assume that if a trade is going to work for you it should work near the beginning. If the trade doesn't reach a predefined level of profit in a certain time period, then you might exit after the time period has passed. Using your MAE you can determine what these levels and time periods should be.

Average Time to Recovery

The number of months it takes you to recover from the low point in your equity decline is your time to recovery. You will experience more than one drawdown in your trading career. The average time to recovery is the average of each of those recoveries.

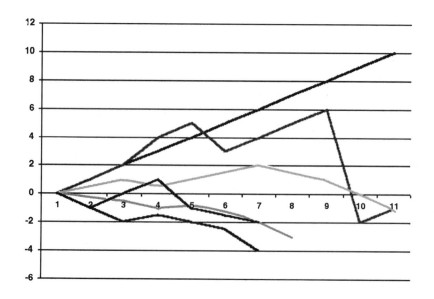

Figure 11.4   Maximum Adverse Excursion

Why is this information important? If your trading seems to be going along great, and you hit a catastrophic drawdown, the significance of that drawdown can be measured by your time to recover. If it only takes you a month to recover, then your loss was not such a big deal. If, however, it takes you the rest of the year to get back to even, then the drawdown was pretty significant.

Now let's say that you've had five periods of drawdown. If the average time to recover from those five was a month or two, you're still an exceptional trader. One bad experience does not ruin your track record, but if the average of all your adverse events is bad, you'd better take another look at your system.

Conclusion

One more thought before moving on. As you design and test your theories, always remember that it takes longer to recover from bad trades than it does to make them. If you lose money on several trades in a row, your bankroll will have decreased. Thus, the power you have to make money is diminished. If your system makes 30 percent per year, you will have reduced the principal upon which you can make that 30 percent. Why am I admonishing you now? Because most of the people who call me for help do so after they've lost much of their money, not before. Do your homework before you trade, not after.

12 FOLLOWING YOUR SYSTEM

Introduction

The most difficult part of trading, without a doubt, is following your system.

If I gave you every rule for my trading methodology, and I told you that it made 100 percent per year, within a matter of weeks you would stop following it. Why? Because you won't have the confidence it takes to withstand the losing periods.

The only way you can gain this confidence is through extensive testing of a system you have either designed yourself or fully understand. You must know every statistic and measurement introduced in this book inside and out. You must be intimately familiar, and comfortable, with how many losing trades you are likely to experience in a row before your system starts winning again.

Even armed with all this information, you will still have trouble following your system. You must bolster your ego and your positive intentions on a daily basis.

Post-it Notes

There are many little tools you can use to keep your focus trained on following your system. Most of these tools are pretty simple, but you'll be surprised how well they work.

Start your own collection of motivational sayings. When you realize you have violated a trading rule, write a positive reinforcement on a Post-it note, and stick it on your monitor. When you find one of those pearls of wisdom in a book, write it on a Post-it note and stick it to your monitor.

Move the notes around every few days, reading each one carefully as you move it. Notes that stay in the same place become part of the surroundings and get ignored.

Hard Hat Area

As a new trader, I found it difficult to stay with my system when it was in drawdown. I knew what my statistics said, I had done all the testing, and I believed it would work. Still, I had a hard time pulling the trigger when the going was tough. I felt like Chicken Little, with the sky falling in around me.

Because I was able to describe my fear as "things falling" (like my equity curve), I decided to go to the hardware store and purchase a hard hat. I even painted my name on the front of the hard hat to make it look official. The investment of time made the object more of a trigger for me. When the going gets tough, I just put on my hard hat and remember to stick with the system.

Buckle Up for Safety

Again, as a new trader, I found that I was attempting to second-guess my system when the market became volatile. If the market was moving fast and I had a decent profit in the trade, I was tempted to take it. If I had a loss in the trade and the market accelerated against me, I was tempted to get out of the trade before the loss became worse.

Forcing myself to pause before overriding my system gave me a few seconds to reconsider my impulse. Creating an anchor to use as a reminder was helpful in this effort. I secured a seat belt to the bottom of my desk chair. Its annoying clang as it dangled against the chair legs served as a constant reminder to follow my rules. Whenever I felt like jumping the gun and overriding my system, I first put on my seat belt. That gave me a moment's pause, and caused me to reflect on my good intentions. That is not to say that I didn't ever override the system. Of course, I did from time to time. But, each time I did, I realized two things: (1) it didn't consistently better my return, and (2) it ruined my ability to track my system's performance.

Conclusion

You can have the best system in the world, but it is of no use if you can't follow it. If you are having trouble in this area, you either need to complete the testing required to give you confidence or seek the help of a trader's coach.

13 THE SCIENCE OF ORGANIZING YOURSELF

Time Management Tools

To-Do List

A "To-Do" list works wonders, simple as it may seem. Avoid using scraps of paper to keep track of something as important as your short-term goal setting! Whether you make a form for yourself, purchase forms at the office supply store, or use your computer, *make your "To-Do" list official.*

Ever the technology nerd, I combine my watch and computer software to minimize the effort and maximize the utility of keeping my To-Do list, schedule, and contacts *all in one place.*

Microsoft offers a program called Schedule+ that is not only broad in spectrum but also easy to use. The program comes with both Microsoft Office and Microsoft Plus! and has a built-in link to the Timex DataLink watch. Figure 13.1 shows a typical daily screen from Schedule+.

On the left side of the screen there are tabs for switching between views: daily, weekly, monthly, planner mode, to-do list, and your phone book. At the same time you view your daily schedule, you can keep track of your list of projects to do and simply click the calendar to move to another date.

From the print menu you can output a hard copy of your

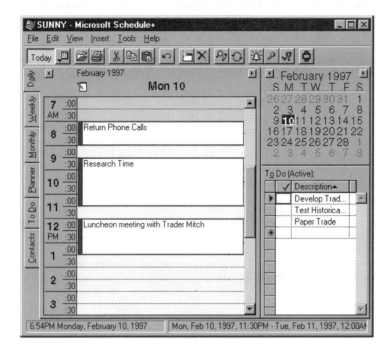

Figure 13.1 Schedule+

schedule in many formats, ranging from phone book to calendar to various time schedule trackers, as in Figure 13.2.

Now for the exciting part! At the top right of the Schedule+ screen is a small button that looks like the face of a watch. Clicking on this icon brings up the utility that transmits my entire set of lists to my Timex DataLink watch, including phone numbers, to-do list, anniversaries, scheduled appointments, alarms, and two time zones. On the face of the watch is an infrared sensor which receives the transmission from my computer screen, via technology much like the bar coding at the grocery store, and stores the information in the watch's memory.

No, I don't get any perks from Microsoft or Timex, nor do I work for them. I simply enjoy sharing the latest in time-saving technology with you.

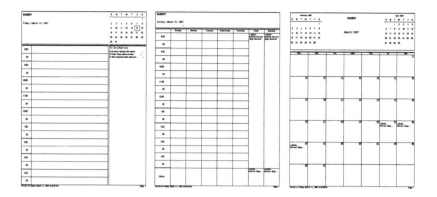

Figure 13.2 Schedule Formats from Schedule+

Whether you keep your to-do list by hand, using a kid's notebook from WalMart, using a DayTimer, on your computer, or in your watch—*keep it! And use it.*

Keeping Track of the Days

There is no single "right" way to keep track of your schedule. There are probably as many ways as there are people. You'll have to do some experimenting so find what suits you best, but here are a few organizing tools I find useful.

There are only so many hours in the day. Let's work backwards on time management just a bit, to help with keeping track of things.

You should allow 8 hours for sleep and relaxation. That leaves 16 hours for other things. You should allow 10 hours for work. That could include commuting, or if you're working at home you can use the extra two hours to get more accomplished. Six hours remain in your theoretical day. Allowing 1½ hours for eating, instead of rushing through meals, gives your body a chance to properly and naturally process the nutritious foods you choose to enhance your health. Using another hour for exercise leaves 3½ hours in your day to spend time with your loved ones, seek enter-

139

tainment, relaxation, or study. It's amazing how much you can accomplish if you structure your days.

Make it a ritual to spend an hour on Sunday night outlining the achievements you would like to complete before next Sunday night. Each morning spend one half hour, using your outline as an overall guide, listing the tasks for today which will move you forward to accomplishing the week's plan. Check off the tasks that you have already completed, preferably as they are done.

Your Hourly Wage

Everything you do has an associated cost. If you want to make $100,000 per year, your net hourly fee is $50. I use estimates, or rough approximations, to make calculations expedient. In this instance, I estimate 2,000 working hours per year (taking out weekends and two weeks for holidays), times $50 equals $100,000. Every hour you spend on the phone costs $50. Every hour you spend talking with co-workers costs $50. Every hour you spend rehashing paperwork costs $50. Your goal is to make each hour pay you $50, not cost you $50! Turn those nonproductive hours into cash. Associate an expense with every task that is done, and assign tasks where you can. If you can make $60 in an hour through trading or studying the markets, paying a clerical person $8 per hour to do your data entry, filing, routing phone calls, and typing puts you out ahead by $2 for that hour.

Every personnel, organization, and time management seminar I've ever attended has stressed that you should try to touch each piece of paper only once. When a bill comes across your desk, pay it or delegate it. When a paper related to a specific project comes across your desk, file it with the project or act on it at the moment. If you maintain a "piling" system instead of a filing system, you will grind your progress wheels to a slow crawl as you hash and rehash each piece of paper again and again.

You will find that in your research and testing of trading systems you must use the most organized procedures you can concoct for each task, or you will become discouraged and not be able to focus on the task at hand.

Since your primary goal is to become a trader, spend most of your time working on trading, not on organizing.

Sorting

In your effort to keep things organized and "touched once," you might find it of benefit to utilize a daily desk file sorter that is numbered from 1 to 31. As you get each piece of correspondence, either take care of it at that moment, or delegate it to the daily file for the day on which it must be done. If the bill is due on the 15th, put it in the section labeled "10," so that you will pay it on the 10th, allowing time for mailing. When you come to the 10th, do it; don't put it off again.

On the front of the daily sorter, tape a copy of this month's calendar. Make notes of important things to do, or keep the calendar in your computer organizer and print it out as part of each morning's half hour ritual.

Better yet, use your sorter to prepare your assistant's work. You look at the bill, approve it, and put it in the sorter for the assistant to pay and mail.

More Sticky Notes (Usually Post-it Notes)

Another hint: sticky notes work great for organizing! Leave yourself a note with each task, so you don't waste time churning when it comes time to do the deed. Once it's done, throw away the note.

If you need an alarm, a time reminder, put it in your watch. Or set an alarm clock. Or, if you carry a personal organizer, put your notes in there and refer to the organizer often. If you have an assistant, have the person remind you of time schedules, and do the deed when the time comes.

My most dreaded task of each day comes at 10 A.M. and again at 2 P.M. My watch sounds the same beep as it does for all the other alarms, but I cringe at the sound when I know it's 10 or

2. At those times I force myself to rise up from my chair, leave my computers, and go for a 15-minute walk. You may enjoy exercise and this may be a valued break for you, but for me it's a chore. Personally, I prefer unbroken concentration of at least six hours' duration, so the exercise break is not welcome for me. Nevertheless, when the alarm goes off I abide by the rules, like it or not.

Some people need to put their tasks and schedules on computer, some need to dictate them to a person or tape recorder, some need to write them down. The only way you will know which method is most successful for you is to try each one, or invent a new one, and see which has the most successful outcome for you.

When you do find the methodology with which you are most comfortable (and most successful), isolate it. Work with one system, not two. (Notice that I've used the word "system" here to refer to your time management recipe.)

Don't duplicate your efforts. Your time management tool must not take time away from you; its purpose is to make your use of time more efficient, and to thereby give you extra time. If you find yourself laboring over your tool, you'll notice that you are spending more time planning than executing. *Get a different tool.* Find the tool that best fits your nature and use it at a specific time each day.

Keep All of Your Organizing Tools in One Place

If you keep your notes and records in a binder (like a DayTimer or DayRunner), be certain that you have adequate forms to keep track of everything from your phone numbers to your checking accounts to your travel arrangements. Don't spend time searching for things. Put it where it belongs immediately. If you use a computerized organizer, be certain to get software that is ample to meet not only your current needs but also expand toward future needs. Until recently I used DayTimer software. However, Microsoft, in its efforts to rule the universe, added Schedule+ and now Outlook to its office package, which provides nearly everything one could think of to facilitate efficiency. And it downloads to the Timex DataLink watch!

Color Schemes

Another great tool for organizing is to design a color scheme that corresponds to your main activities. If you maintain this color scheme throughout your business, you can tell at a glance in which category each activity belongs. Use colored markers, colored highlighters, colored pens, colored files, and colored stickies according to your designated scheme.

For instance, I use pink for everything which has to do with my trading. I have pink file folders, pink paper, pink notebooks, pink envelopes, and pink markers. When it comes to papers, correspondence, and tasks related to *Traders' Catalog & Resource Guide* (my quarterly magazine) I use yellow for everything. Guess what color bills are in: red! And my *Money Mentor* internet activities are all blue. I have many more colors assigned, but you get the idea by now.

When I travel, I keep a single folder in which I accumulate my travel plans, tickets, an expense report sheet and envelope, contact names and numbers, and maps of my destination. I find that a cellular phone is a cost savings when traveling: I can call the office to assign activities or collect important messages, and I can leave messages for myself on the answering machine when I have those spontaneous ideas that just can't wait.

Organizing Your Trading Ideas

In your planner, whether it be notebook or computer, designate a section for trading ideas. You never know when the light will flash. Write your theory down, along with any notes about how to execute and test it. That way it is not a lingering "to do" cluttering up your mind, or one which will be forgotten by the time you get around to testing.

Space Planning

Make the best use of your office space. Even if your workspace is small, it can be organized efficiently to allow for maximum productivity. If you don't have enough space, or it isn't well organized, you will find yourself losing things, buying new things, and constantly shuffling things around. Visit your local organizer store or take a look at the Home Office Catalog. Companies like Anthro and Wall Street Trading Desks offer space-saving furniture that can help you in your organizing and decorating at the same time.

Remove dust-gathering piles from your immediate work area and relegate them to storage boxes or to the bookshelves. Things you don't use daily, put farthest away from you. Materials that you use on a daily basis, keep within immediate reach.

Computer Power

Consider purchasing more than one computer. While today's computers ostensibly multitask, they still have wait times. While you are waiting for a task to complete, often you are unable to execute any other tasks on that computer. For this reason, I like to have several computers.

I never put any software on my trading computer, other than the software I use directly for trading. Any tools that are used for research and testing reside on a separate computer for safety's sake. Furthermore, while running an extended test on my number crunching computer, I don't want to sit there and watch the hard drive spin. I have yet another computer to keep financial information and my time-management and contact-management tools. I guess you can tell I don't like to waste time.

Quick Reference

Post important numbers in strategic places. For instance, put the number for the copier repair service on the copier. Put your broker's phone number either on the phone or on your trading computer's monitor. And be sure to keep all your other important numbers in your "little black book," no matter what form it takes. For each and every piece of hardware or software I purchase, I keep the date of purchase, where I purchased it, the serial number and password, and all the relevant phone numbers in one record in my contact management software.

Your Trading Records

As you test your theories, and subsequently as you begin trading, you will generate massive amounts of paper. Keeping track of what it all means can become a full-time job.

Like using separate computers, I like to use separate file cabinets. I keep all of my testing theories and results in a location away from other kinds of paperwork.

Document each test or set of tests, before you run them and after you run them. First document what you are going to do, and then document the results of what you did. Remember, you are a researcher, and you don't want to prejudice your outcomes with preconceived notions. Next year, or the year after, when you come back to review your efforts, you will have forgotten what you did. If you have kept an accurate record, you will be able to reconstruct your thought process and avoid duplicating your effort.

It is often helpful to create an index or table of contents to your filing system, so you can find things by glancing rather than rummaging.

Keep another file cabinet or drawer for your trading confirmations, statements, and account balances. Your real-time trading results will be important to you for several reasons, not the least of which is taxes. You will want to keep summaries of your real-time trading results, which will include weekly, monthly, or annual results in a tabular format.

Your real-time results will be important to you if you ever want to manage money for someone else. They will also be important for you to compare to your theoretical performance.

Keep all your trading results together in one place. And, keep them organized.

Income and Outgo

In another section, drawer or drawers, keep your accounts receivable and accounts payable. In the beginning of your trading business you may not have any accounts receivable, but create the section anyway. Keep careful track of all your receipts and become acutely aware of the balance between your spending and your trading income.

Establish your bill-paying practice. When a bill comes in, pay it or schedule it for payment. Use your 1-31 divider system for your bills, as well as your correspondence. Don't use the piling system.

Taxes

Taxation for traders can be a complicated issue. Most tax accountants are well qualified to deal with long-term investors, but not versed in the nuances of frequent traders. Choose your accountant carefully through an interviewing process. Ted Tesser, (see Appendix F) of Waterside Financial, has written books on how to deal with the tax obligations you will face as a trader. You would do well to read his works, including *The Serious Investor's Tax Survival Guide.*

Summary

In short, be as efficient as you can possibly imagine. As your business grows, and you become more and more busy, the efficiency will more than pay for your initial effort.

14 THE SCIENCE OF THE BUSINESS

Introduction

Trading is a very serious business. This endeavor can become all-consuming (with more tentacles than an octopus) encompassing your personal time as well as your allotted work time.

Trading is the only business I know of which pays you sometimes and you pay it at other times. With most jobs you can expect a paycheck; with trading you can lose everything you have!

There is only one goal in trading: to make money. Certainly an important element of your business will be that you enjoy what you do, but you can enjoy your efforts and not make a profit. When treating it like a business, every step you take must be to further your primary goal: making money.

When you consider purchasing another computer, ask whether it will add to or subtract from the business' bottom line. When you want another piece of trading software, ask whether it will add to or subtract from the bottom line. When you begin looking at new offices, ask whether it will add to or subtract from the bottom line. Often we busy ourselves with the trappings and forget that the bottom line is of prime importance.

A new camera does not make you a better photographer. The purchase of new trading software, office equipment, and business trappings will not make you a better trader. Hard work and study will improve your photography and your trading skills. Consider adding to your education before adding to your inventory.

Make your plan and stick to it. Set out your goals for this business as you would for any other business. Create long-term time lines for expansion based on "worst-case" scenarios, rather than "pie-in-the-sky" hopeful scenarios. Be detailed in your specifications, pretending that you must present your plan to your banker, or a venture capitalist for funding.

This chapter will talk about the how-to's of making your own business plan.

Getting Down to Business

One of the main reasons that traders fail is not their lack of trading skills but their lack of business skills. Traders aren't the only ones who suffer from this dilemma. Physicians, in medical school, receive an enormous amount of scientific information but very little information about running their practice from a business standpoint. Young attorneys are taught to argue the law but not to run a business. This is true of most technical schooling.

Having the best education and talent for your current or previous profession is not enough to guarantee your success in trading. You might be a highly trained attorney, or accountant, or engineer, and have been tremendously successful at it, but that does not insinuate that you will become equally as successful as a trader.

To become a successful trader, plan on spending as much time obtaining the appropriate education for the job as you would spend becoming educated for any other profession.

If you plan to run a successful trading business, in addition to developing a proven, profitable trading system, you must develop the skills of running a business, which requires just as much education as you devoted to your current profession.

Many doctors and lawyers, as well as money managers, sadly make the mistake of assuming that their professional training as a physician, attorney, or engineer ensures them of success in their new business. If you doubt the truth of this statement, a trip to the bankruptcy court will make you a believer in the importance of having an education in running a professional business.

Business Reality Check

Last year alone, according to a press release from the United States bankruptcy courts, over 1,800,000 people declared bankruptcy in the United States. In southern California alone there were 80,000 bankruptcies. These figures include personal bankruptcies but do not include the businesses that just fizzled out because of lack of interest, mismanagement, or being undercapitalized. Nationally over 90 percent of new businesses fail within the first year, and of those surviving 10 percent only 30 percent continue after three years. So, based on statistics, you will only have a 3 percent chance of creating a business that will withstand the test of time. To beat the odds you must at least start with a fighting chance by having the tools necessary for success, the first being a plan of action.

Setting Goals

All too often I hear wanna-be traders saying that they expect to generate 100 percent plus profits through trading. They've heard stories about traders like Hillary, who turn $1,000 into $100,000, and think that this is exactly what will happen to them. Since Hillary did it, they believe they too can read the *Wall Street Journal* and get rich.

Please don't set this as your goal. Be realistic. There are several ways to form realistic trading goals by asking yourself some common sense questions. What does an average retail business make? What does the average professional trader make? What does the Dow Jones Industrial Average make? What does the S&P 500 Index make?

The Average Retail Business

What would you expect to make as net profit if you started up a new business with a product to sell?

All too often you forget that trading is a business and act more like gamblers. Remember that this is your new, start-up business and treat it as such.

Let's set our business net profit target at that of the average business in the United States. Surfing through the Internet, I came to a recent report from the U.S. Bureau of the Census stating, "For the third quarter of 1996 . . . the annual rate of after-tax return on stockholders' equity was 12.0 percent." That's reasonable; let's use that as our goal. (In case you are wondering, the Web site is http://www.census.gov).

Therefore, if your after-expenses trading profits are 12 percent or higher, you are doing as well as the average American business. That would be a reasonable goal for a new trader. Furthermore, it is a difficult, though attainable, target. Sure, there are a few traders who make it to the 100 percent annual level. There are also a few athletes who make it to the olympics.

Okay. Enough of that diversion. Let's get back to comparative measures of success.

The Dow Jones Industrial Average

Our final index of comparison examines the most commonly known statistics. The Dow Jones Industrial Average is a collection of 30 stocks which presumably represents the economy. Introduced in 1896 by Charles H. Dow, it originally included only 12 stocks, and of those 12 only General Electric remains as a Dow stock today. Originally the index contained American Cotton Oil, American Sugar, American Tobacco, Chicago Gas, Distilling and Cattle Feeding, Laclede Gas, National Lead, North American, Tennessee Coal and Iron, US Leather, and US Rubber. Now the index is comprised of companies like IBM and McDonalds.

Your stockbroker will tell you that a buy-and-hold approach to investing will in the long run net you more return than any other scheme. How many times have I heard ". . . a $10,000 investment 25 years ago would currently be worth $802,000."

Let's see what it would take for us to do as well as the Dow Jones Industrial Average. A list of the 30 stocks which comprise the DJIA are in Appendix A if you're interested. Also in Appendix C is the annual data for the DJIA from which I calculated this information. (See Figure 14.1.)

Averaging the returns of each year, from 1951 through 1996, shows us that over the past thirty-something years the Dow Jones Industrial Average has averaged 9 percent annually. By this measure, if you were to consistently do better than the Dow, you'd be making 10 percent or more each year.

Your Measures of Success

None of these averages, DJIA, CTAs, or Retail Business, takes into account the potential affect of compounding. All I've done is look at each year separately. Compounding the averages, that is leaving all the money in the account and increasing the trade quantities is a money management technique. You will want to study the effects of compounding on your risk and reward. Consider, in your measurements, that if you are trading for a living, you probably will not leave all of your profits in the business for long periods. You probably will want to take money out to live on.

The bottom line here is that very few traders or money managers make more than 10 percent per year. I tell you this, not to discourage you from trading, but to keep you encouraged when

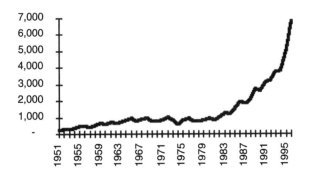

Figure 14.1 Dow Jones Industrial Average 1951–1996

your returns are average. Go ahead and aim for the 100 percent star, but don't indulge in the fantasy that it's easy to get there.

Planning Your Business

Money, Money, Money

Trading capital is one of your business assets; it is your inventory. Do not confuse your trading capital with your office expenses, nor with your personal finances. They must be kept very separate in your mind and in your accounting.

Do not confuse your trading profits with your net profits. You are running a small business, remember? Your trading profits are your gross profits, from which you must subtract your expenses. Data doesn't come to you for free and neither does a computer. Taxes and telephone are additional expenses you must consider. Let's break the components of your business into budget items so that you can analyze income and expenses.

Costly Shortcuts

There are essentials in your business, around which you probably should not try to make shortcuts. Both in the long- and the short-run these tools will be time savers for you and thus save you money.

A good answering machine can act as a substitute for a receptionist for a long time. This is especially true if you have a computer you can devote to answering the phone, so you can assign voice-mail boxes to segregate functions like requests for information, trading fills, and personal calls. Telephony applications like SuperVoice and Visual Voice are comparatively inexpensive and act as a great buffer for filtering out distractions.

A clerical person to do your filing, typing, errands, and data entry can increase your efficiency an order of magnitude. In the beginning you probably won't need this person full-time, so contact a local temp agency and get someone to come in two afternoons a week. It's too easy for you to confuse being busy with productivity. Spending your time doing clerical functions makes you feel like you worked hard but doesn't get you further along in your research and trading.

Your computer equipment is your main tool. If you are trying to force an old clunker to do the job for which you need a Pentium, you will be spending most of your time acting as a hardware expert. A used or reconditioned monitor can be bought for $80, and a new Pentium with all the bells and whistles can be as little as $800, if you have a repair shop built it for you from parts. Buy two; they're cheap.

Your market data is probably the last place you should cut corners. As they say, garbage in, garbage out. If you feed your system inaccurate data, you will be getting erroneous results upon which you intend to base your entire business. How smart is that? Don't get your data from your friends. Rely on highly reputable data vendors and pay for their best service. Don't cut corners here!

Budgeting

As a philosopher, statistician, and armchair psychologist, I have noticed that the folks who start a new business by renting prime office space and furnishing it with the best of the best are usually out of that office within a year. The cautious new entrepreneur who begins in the garage, on the other hand, and accumulates furnishings (often used) as needed, taking on only those expenses his profits will cover is far more likely to succeed in the long run.

There is a delicate balance between being extravagant and being parsimonious. As Benjamin Franklin said, "Penny wise, pound foolish." If you base your business plan on savings, rather than increasing income, you are planning backwards. Likewise, never base your investing plan on the tax man. You are a trader! That means you are a profit-motivated capitalist. If you spend your efforts determining means of generating profits, the expenses (including taxes) will take care of themselves.

Avoid poverty consciousness. Take stock of your "musts" and your "wants." Adequate desk space and a comfortable chair are important; plush surroundings are not. Having a computer with enough power and storage that you can get your research done without fighting the hardware is imperative; having the latest, greatest, top of the line computer is not.

And paramount in your planning: *don't spend money you don't have.* Trading is not likely to produce a steady monthly income, especially in the beginning. It has its ups and downs. Look back at Figure 8.2 of the VAMI for the average CTA. There are months with no income. In fact, there are months with negative income. So, don't go out on a limb and get loans (or even extend yourself loans via credit cards) against income you anticipate but don't yet have.

Assign a dollar value to your own time. There are occasions when it is inappropriate for you to do the work yourself. If you know what the value of your own time is, you can more easily determine these occasions. For instance, let's say that your goal is to make $100,000 your first year, and that to do so, you must do the research, testing, and trading yourself. Using an estimated 2,000 hours per year, your time is worth $50 per hour. Every task you do which takes you away from your stated priorities is an expense to the company. If you do the filing and answering the telephone, and you spend three hours a day doing it, you are costing the company $150 per day, by getting behind in your scheduled goal. You will end the year being 750 hours behind or $37,500 away from your goal. You would be better off paying a temp service $10 per hour to do your clerical work, while you concentrate on your primary goal. Always aim toward making the highest and best use of your time. Your time is your most expensive commodity.

Income

Anticipate and plan; set your goals high and your expectations low. Try to be realistic and at the same time hopeful.

If you want to make a million dollars a year, that's not unreasonable, just break that goal down into its daily equivalent. Having done that, then begin to analyze what it would take to generate that much income on a daily basis, above your expenses. This process is very similar to finding your PHW in Chapter 6.

154

At every step along the way you must ask "What does it take?" and "Am I willing to do what it takes?"

Assuming you take weekends off and two weeks per year for vacation, there are then 250 working days in a year. To make a million dollars in that year you must produce a net profit of $4,000 each and every day. Above your losses! If one day you lose $2,000, the next day you must make $6,000. Breaking this down a bit further, if you can make $500 per day net trading one S&P contract, then you must trade eight contracts to make a million dollars in a year. Eight S&P contracts, at today's $15,000 margin requirement would be $120,000 in your account, just to cover the margin. I recommend having a minimum of twice the margin in your account before you even think about trading, which would mean you would need $240,000 to make your million. That is, if you can find a sure way to make $500 per contract to start with.

Whatever your goal, keep a progress chart. If you want to establish a workout program, keep a log of your routine and when you increase repetitions, frequency, or weight in your training. If you want to lose weight, make a chart for the year, with realistic weight milestones, and plot your actual weight against it daily. If you want to make a million dollars a year, keep a chart of your goal and plot your actual progress on a weekly basis toward that goal. (See Figure 14.2.)

Some weeks your dot will be over the line, some weeks it will be under. But, as long as you are making progress in the right direction and staying near your goal line, you are doing the right thing.

Outgo

In any business you will have fixed costs (FC) and variable costs (VC). Fixed costs remain the same month after month, independent of how many widgets you make or how many trades you take. Variable costs vary directly with the number of widgets or trades. For instance, commission is a variable cost, which rises and falls according to the number of contracts or shares you are

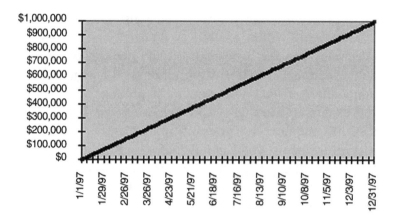

Figure 14.2 How to Make a Million Dollars in a Year

trading. Your rent is a fixed cost, staying the same every month, regardless of how much you trade.

Your total costs (TC) are the sum of your fixed costs and your variable costs. Your breakeven point (BE) is where your total costs are equal to your total income. In analyzing your business and its potential for success, you will need to find your breakeven point. How much trading profit must you bring in to cover all your costs? How much trading capital is necessary to generate this trading profit?

Expense Worksheet

Keep yourself honest. Write down your estimates of your business' monthly fixed and variable expenses. Figures 14.3 and 14.4 provide a format that should help in this effort.

What other expenses are you likely to incur? Keep careful track of your ledgers, either by hand, using spreadsheet software, or using an accounting program like Quicken or QuickBooks.

Your Trading Business Plan

There are many ways you can get help structuring a basic business plan. Every bookstore carries several books on the subject,

Item	Monthly Expense
Your Salary	$3,000
Wages for Temp Help	$1,000
Rent	$1,000
Utilities	$300
Telephone	$300
Insurance	$100
Shipping & Postage	$100
Data Service Fees	$300
Taxes & Licenses	$100
Legal Fees	$100
Accounting Fees	$100
TOTAL ESTIMATED FIXED COSTS	$6,400

Figure 14.3   Fixed Costs

Item	Monthly Expense
Travel	
Seminars & Conferences	
Education & Books	
Magazine Subscriptions	
Office Supplies	
Computer Maintenance & Upgrades	
Software	
Historical Data	
TOTAL ESTIMATED VARIABLE COSTS	

Figure 14.4   Variable Costs

157

including formats you can mimic. Jian software makes a combined book and software product, called BizPlanBuilder, which will walk you through the process step by step. Browsing the Internet, you will be able to find both shareware and retail software to help you get more ideas for your business plan. Two great sites for shareware downloads are http://www.download.com and http://www.zdnet.com. If you're looking to purchase retail software at a discount, my most recent venture is into a Yellow Pages Directory and Web site for software. It's called the "Big Yellow Software Book." Come visit me online at http://www.bysb.com.

The Essentials of Any Business Plan

Your business plan accomplishes two things: it gets you to organize your plan and it gets the plan into a conventional form with which businesspeople are familiar.

A business plan for traders follows the standard guidelines, except that your product is not tangible.

Generally accepted business plans have these essential ingredients:

1. Cover page
2. Table of contents
3. Mission statement
4. About the company
5. About the marketplace
6. Company differentiators
7. Time lines, milestones, and deadlines
8. Goals and objectives
9. Resource requirements
10. Financial plan
11. Risks and rewards
12. Summary

One of your objectives in creating this business plan is to make it pretty. Microsoft has done the world a great favor by creating standardized templates in its Microsoft Office products, which make it easy for even the most graphically challenged people to create pretty reports. There is no excuse for sloppy formatting, when Microsoft has done it all for you.

Cover Page

Using one of the formats from Microsoft Word (contemporary, professional, elegant), create a front page for your "report." This page should remain simple and uncluttered, containing just the name of your company (if it has one), the date of the plan, your name and position, and the address information about the company.

Table of Contents

What can I say about this one? Name the sections of your report and assign a page number to each page. Make a list of each section with its corresponding page number. If you use one of the Microsoft templates, you can leave the table of contents until last and have MS Word do it for you.

Mission Statement

Also known as the goals or statement of purpose, in this section you need to clearly state your goals. What do you plan to achieve and why? Be concise and use words that will help direct the growth of your enterprise but don't go overboard.

You might want to give a broad brushstroke overview of your goals for the next five years, without going into the details.

Your goal, if you agree with what you've read in this book, is to make money. You probably intend to do this through honest and ethical means by supplying liquidity to the markets by way of trading [fill in the blank]. Your mission is to create a comfortable [living, retirement, adjunct to your current lifestyle] through successfully trading your system. Paramount in that effort is the creation of a profitable trading system, which will be the thrust of your first [fill in the blank] months of effort. Having designed and tested the system, proving that all statistics point to the likelihood of this system producing a profit, you will then embark on maintaining the discipline necessary to follow your methodology.

Figure 14.5 includes a chart and/or spreadsheet of your long-range goals.

About the Company

In this section you present your company's history, including that of the management team. You should include previous accomplishments to show your successes and summarize your years of experience. If the company is only you, you will be summarizing your resume in this section. If you have any prior trading history, you will want to discuss your track record.

This is also the section to talk about your company structure, now and any plans for the future. You may just be a single-person enterprise now, but you should plan for additions of support staff as you grow.

Your present situation is appropriately discussed in this section. What are you doing currently for income? What is the size of your nest egg and how much are you willing to risk and leave a losing to this business? (Please remember that all trading is risky; you should only trade with money you are willing to lose.)

If you are including any financial or management partners in this venture, this is the place to champion their strengths, education, and experience.

	Year 1	Year 2	Year 3	Year 4
P/L	$ (10,000)	$ 10,000	$ 30,000	$ 50,000

Figure 14.5   Long-Range Trading Goals

About the Marketplace

What is your product? To what audience can it be marketed? Who are your potential customers? Do you have any competition? What is the risk of this venture?

These questions are addressed in the typical business plan, for a typical business. Since you already know you are atypical, you are going to modify this section heavily for your own purposes.

As traders, our product is our trading system. You are your own audience, unless you plan to market your trading system to outsiders. Your trading system may be adapted for one or several market vehicles; you may be interested in stocks or you may be interested in commodities.

This is the section to use for talking about your system, its design and purpose.

Clearly specify your trading rules. If you are going to show this plan to others, you may want to have a pull-out section that you can keep private, for your eyes only. Whatever form it takes, be sure to include the following:

- Setup rules
- Entry rules
- Profit taking rules
- Exit rules
- Stop loss rules
- Portfolio and money management algorithms

Company Differentiations

How is your plan different from all the rest of the thousands of traders in the world? How will you stack up against the professionals? Why do you think you are better off doing it yourself than letting a professional manage your money for you? What about your trading system, methodology, or discipline makes your product viable?

This is a good place to include statistics (like those mentioned in this book) about your system. Compare your actual or hypothetical performance to that of the market and/or to other traders.

Time Lines, Milestones, and Deadlines

Now is the time for you to come to grips with the time line and exact testing procedures you will use as you struggle through the jungle of concepts and designs leading you toward the Holy Grail.

For you to actually achieve a goal, you must have a goal. The more definite you are about time schedules and milestones, the more likely you are to actually achieve the goal.

Just as you have been exacting about stating your trading rules, use this section to be as precise with your testing guidelines.

Goals and Objectives

How far do you want to go? How realistic is it? How do you get from here to there?

Remember from earlier in this chapter how to make a million dollars in a year? It's as simple as setting well-defined goals and "doing what it takes." Let's look at an example that's a tad more reasonable to start with. I'll leave the million-dollar part to you. Let's see how to make $100,000 per year.

Estimating that there are 2,000 hours in a working year, you can quickly say that you will need to make $50 per hour to achieve the goal. If you work eight hours per day, you need to turn $400 profit per day to make your plan work. If you are trading a 45 percent profitable system, that means you need approximately $900 per day in profitable trades, because you will experience a $500 loss per day. Structuring your goal as clearly as that will get you to the goal a lot faster.

Let's look at those estimates in spreadsheet form as shown in Figure 14.6.

Year 1	Jan	Feb	Mar	Apr	May	Jun
Trade P/L	8334	8334	8334	8334	8334	8334

	Jul	Aug	Sep	Oct	Nov	Dec	TOTAL
	8334	8334	8334	8334	8334	8334	100000

Figure 14.6   Month by Month for the First Year

Keeping track of your progress in this same spreadsheet will keep you motivated to step up your efforts if you are behind, and it will reward you psychologically when you are ahead of schedule.

Resource Requirements

You will need any number of tools and resources for the ultimate accomplishment of your trading plan. The list of tools will be dependent upon your methods of trading.

At a minimum you will need information, a brokerage account, a telephone, a calculator, pencils, and paper. If you plan to computerize your efforts you must provide for the purchase, lease or amortization of a computer, and the software requisite for your plan.

Look back at the expenses worksheet earlier in this chapter. Be certain that you have accounted for all potential avenues of expense likely to affect your bottom line.

Discuss these expenses in this section and include detailed spreadsheets showing month by month "outgo."

Financial Plan

Your financial plan will include a full analysis of the information you put together relating to Figures 14.3 and 14.4. Include both a short-range and a long-range plan in this section.

163

Incorporate into your spreadsheets (or tables) your current assets, your expenses, your potential or anticipated income, and a full breakeven analysis.

Your long-range plan should provide an analysis of the potential you have for the next five years, at a minimum. Make this analysis on a year by year basis. Your short-range plan should cover the next 12 months on a month by month basis.

Risks and Rewards

By now you have done so much introspection and inspection that you may wonder whether there are any rewards to this venture. Of course there are, for the diligent and hard working few who persist. As I said, there is no Holy Grail, and this is not a get-rich-quick pursuit.

In this section of your business plan you should fully analyze the pros and cons, the risks and rewards, and evaluate whether this is really a sound entrepreneurial strategy. If your plan shows more risk than reward, consider revising your system or your capital outlay.

Summary

Now is the time to put it all together. In a few short paragraphs, "say what you said." When a screenwriter goes in to a producer or director to sell an idea for a new movie, he or she is allowed 5 minutes and 100 words to "pitch" the concept. Make this section your pitch. If you can't say it all in 100 words, you don't understand your business yet. Go back to the Japanese brainstorming technique section of this book and define your question. A clear definition of the question will give you the answer.

That's It

That is all there is to it. Once your business plan is clear to you, the accomplishment of the task outlined therein will be much easier. Make it pretty. Spend the time to put it into one of the Microsoft

Word templates and print it out. You might even run down to Kinko's and have them bind it for you.

Refer back to your business plan at least monthly. Compare the reality of your execution to the plan you set forth. Write in actual expenses and profits. Keep charts of your progress. And if you are doing well, let me hear from you.

15 DEALING WITH PSYCHOLOGICAL ISSUES

Adrienne Laris Toghraie, MNLP, MCH

Adrienne Toghraie is president and founder of Trading on Target and Enriching Life Seminars. She is a Master Practitioner of Neuro-Linguistic Programming, a Master Time-Line Therapist and a Master Hypnotherapist. Over the last nine years Adrienne has specialized in coaching people in the investment field to their next level of success. Adrienne's articles have been featured in financial magazines and newsletters internationally. She has appeared as a keynote speaker at industry conferences as well as being a featured guest on television programs. Adrienne's newest books, *The Winning Edge 2—Traders' and Investors Psychological Coach in a Book* and *Dear Coach—Potty Training for Traders, Brokers and Investors,* have received high praise from financial magazines and newsletters. For more information, feel free to contact Ms. Toghraie at Trading on Target, 100 Lavewood Ln, Cary, NC 27511. Phone 919-851-8288, fax 919-851-9979, e-mail adtoghraie@ aol.com.

Trading is a mirror that reflects back to you what you are ready to receive.

Discipline in following your own rules is the key to success in trading. You can easily determine your level of discipline by your trading results, provided you have a good system or methodology. If you are successful and are making money consistently, you are disciplined. If you do not or cannot follow your rules, you will be among the majority of traders who lose money in the markets. Most traders lose money because they fall into psychological traps that are a result of how they have programmed their minds throughout their lives. An individual's programming is determined by how he perceives life. Your perceptions are a comfortable habit that will determine the thoughts you think, the actions you take, and the resulting outcomes that lead to your success or failure. Unless there is a transformation (change in perception), you can depend upon your present patterns and habits to be the same for the rest of your life. If your perceptions lead you to the kind of action in which you cannot follow your trading rules, you will suffer the consequence of sabotaged efforts.

In this chapter, you will find the psychological traps into which traders fall and specific strategies to pull yourself out of those traps. Many, if not most, of these traps have their origin in unresolved past issues. In this chapter I will only briefly allude to these issues as this is a vast area of study that will be covered in a future book.

While I have studied many psychological sciences, I prefer the technique of neuro-linguistic programming (NLP). NLP is also known as the science of modeling. What makes it attractive to me is that the techniques are fast and effective and creates the least amount of emotional discomfort for the client.

Several traditional NLP, as well as other, strategies will be presented to apply on your own in this chapter. While they might seem simple, they are highly effective when applied.

I have included a self-evaluation so you can direct your attention to those psychological traps which are relevant to you at this time.

Self-Evaluation for Sabotage Traps in Your Trading

The following evaluation will give you insight into whether you are sabotaging your trading and falling into psychological traps. Answer each statement with a true or false response.

I. Preparation

1. I do not have a specific plan of action for my trading and/ or my business.
2. I have chosen a trading system that is not suited to my personality or my optimum time frame for trading.
3. I jumped into trading without adequate study, preparation, testing, and/or capital.
4. I decided to trade intuitively before I learned how to trade successfully with a mechanical system.
5. I have gotten into trading for the excitement.

II. Motivation

1. I do not believe my system or methodology and/or my ability as a trader will ultimately earn me money.
2. I am bored with my life and with trading.
3. I lack energy and vitality.
4. I dread the thought of trading each day.
5. I find it hard to take action, so I give myself excuses for not trading. As a result, I find myself putting off doing the things I need to do for my trading.

III. Conflicts

1. I am in constant conflict about my trading decisions.
2. My parents/spouse want me to be in a different profession, and they are disappointed that I am trading. I can hear their voices of disappointment in my mind.
3. I experienced a painful loss in my life, and as a result, I am afraid of additional loses.
4. I seem to reach a ceiling in my trading that I can't break through.

5. I am withholding communication of my true feelings to those closest to me.

IV. Emotional States

1. I stop following my trading rules when I have just lost money in the markets or when I am in a trade and I am afraid that I am going to lose money.
2. I feel an overwhelming sense of power after a series of windfall trades, and as a result, do not follow my rules.
3. I am prone to temper outbursts and feel angry at the market as though it is a person trying to hurt me.
4. I feel terribly guilty about the results of my trading.
5. I worry a lot.
6. I feel a great deal of sorrow because of painful experiences in my life.

V. Losses and Wins

1. I am afraid to enter trades for fear of taking any more losses.
2. I am afraid of the responsibility I might have to assume if I created more earnings.
3. I sometimes feel relieved when I take a loss after a series of winning trades.
4. I associate winning with a sense of loss.

VI. Perceptions

1. I do not believe that I deserve to make a great deal of money, and I feel uncomfortable when I make too much.
2. I believe that in order to succeed I must work long, hard hours and I can't allow myself to relax or take time off from my trading.
3. I believe that trading has no real value and makes no contribution to society.

VII. Negative Behaviors

1. I am consumed by my trading and do not have a balanced life.

2. I abuse my body with the consumption of addictive and energy draining substances.
3. I make agreements with others and with myself and then I fail to keep them.
4. I abuse my mind with negative and critical self-talk.
5. I am constantly complaining or physically ill.
6. I cannot follow my system. (This statement is true if any of the following are true:)
7. I enter trades too late or not at all.
8. I am inconsistent about my rules for using stops.
9. I exit too early or too late.
10. I risk too much or too little.
11. I change my rules.
12. I do not take responsibility for my rules.
13. I try to outguess the markets.
14. I let outside distractions interfere with my trading decisions.
15. I am in a continuous state of disorganization.
16. I never take vacations or reward myself for my successes and good efforts.
17. I feel a need to be in control of everything in my life, especially the markets.
18. I am uncomfortable when everything in my life is not perfect.

VIII. Environmental Issues

1. I have just experienced a major change in my life (new marriage, new baby, new job, new house, etc.)
2. My spouse and I constantly fight over my trading.
3. I am under a tremendous amount of stress in my life.
4. My working and/or living environment is too noisy, quiet, dark, cold, hot, crowded, depressing, uncomfortable, chaotic, and so forth. It is polluted by cigarette smoke, chemical smells and emissions, too much electric current, mold, substances to which I am allergic, and so forth.

The Eight Major Psychological Traps for Traders and the Strategies for Overcoming Them

A "true" response to any of the following statements indicates a high probability that you have fallen into one of these traps and are unwittingly sabotaging your efforts to reach your best performance. Please note the categories in which you have true answers and refer to them in the appropriate section for an understanding of the causes as well as strategies for dealing with these traps or avoiding them when possible.

Trap 1: Lack of Preparedness

If you are not psychologically prepared to trade, you will fall into the first trap. (Please refer to other sections of the book for more details on this first area.) Instead of taking all of the steps necessary to ensure success, you will sabotage your trading career by not being psychologically prepared and therefore will not have the right foundation.

Following are some common problems experienced by traders who are not psychologically prepared to trade.

Problem 1. The Trader without a Business Plan

The very first thing a new business owner must do is prepare a detailed business plan. Without a plan, a trader easily becomes lost in the web of details and responsibilities that a new career entails. Their financial situation will easily spin out of control, and the trader will have difficulty attracting and keeping investors. The lack of control creates stress, which affects trading. Without a plan a trader will be mentally disorganized and unfocused about the goals and therefore will limit any success.

For all the necessary information to develop a good business trading plan, refer to the first part of this book. Remember that a good plan is only good if you follow it.

Problem 2. The Mismatched Trader

It is important to select a trading system, a trading venue, and/or a time frame that is matched to your personality and resources. If you are not trading to your potential, ask yourself the following questions:

1. Under what conditions do I seem to do my best and feel my best?
2. Do I work well alone or do I need to be around people?
3. What part of trading do I find stressful and what about it do I really enjoy?
4. What could I change about the way I trade that would make me feel happier, less stressed?
5. With what time frame for trading do I feel most comfortable?
6. Do I have enough capital to trade my system and earn the profits I need to earn at this time?

These questions and others that relate to your mode of trading might reveal a serious mismatch that, if corrected, will point you in the right direction to successful trading.

Problem 3. The Too-Soon Trader

The trader who does not take the time to learn about the markets, to develop and test a system because of overenthusiasm will pay a price in emotional and financial wreckage. Immediate gratification to make profits and enjoy the excitement of the game is what they want. This category also includes those traders who do not put aside an adequate amount of capital for trading. Not enough capital will result in risks that are too high, not enough money to earn a living or scared trading money.

Problem 4. The Too-Soon Intuitive/Discretionary Trader

Whether you want to be a mechanical or intuitive/discretionary trader, you must still acquire and apply the same foundation of knowledge as discussed in *Trading 101* and *Trading 102* before you will earn a consistent living in the trading business.

Problem 5. The Excitement-Junkie Trader

Most traders go into trading because they enjoy the addiction to high emotional states. They need to feel this excitement and high drama because of unresolved past traumatic experiences. For this reason, it is important to handle these negative issues before starting to trade or you will continue to trade for the wrong reasons. Trauma issues must be worked out with a professional.

Trap 2: Lack of Motivation

If you are not the kind of person to be a continuous self-motivator, this second trap will be one to which you will be highly vulnerable.

Some of the major problems experienced by traders who suffer from a lack of motivation include:

Problem 1. Inability to Take Action

Confidence in one's ability to make money in the markets is a key motivator for a trader. A trader who does not trust his system or his ability will be unable to take action when there is a good setup. What will appear to be a lack of motivation will actually be a lack of confidence.

An effective way to increase your confidence is to learn to listen to your self-talk for negative, self-defeating messages that make you want to give up. Then restate these negative messages into positive messages. An example would be, "I don't have what it takes to become a professional trader." Translation: "If others can become top traders, so can I because the same skills are available to me."

Problem 2. Boredom

Many traders enjoy the developmental stage of trading but find it boring to follow the rules of a system because it is routine and mechanical to do so. These traders were motivated by the creativity of the developmental stage but do not find any creativity in following their mechanical system. One solution would be to continue to do research developing another system while following the rules of your moneymaking system.

Problem 3. Lack of Energy and Vitality

When traders face the reality that it takes time to develop trading skills, they very often do not have the energy and passion to push through the constant obstacles that the trading business can present. In order to feel energy and passion, you must allow the creative side of your brain to be constantly stimulated. Most traders are left-brained, which means they are very technically oriented. And, while trading is technically stimulating, the creative right side of your brain is what will excite the passion necessary to keep you motivated. A trader who does not feel passion for the craft will not be excited about the challenge of each new day.

One of the most effective ways to develop passion is by visualizing the details associated with enjoying the process of reaching your goals. With each step forward, visualize the rewards that success brings to you and the significant people in your life. It is important to add as much detail as possible. You will know that you have accomplished this when you are emotionally excited and feel an added boost of energy that propels you forward.

Problem 4. Trader Anxiety

It is difficult for a trader to start the day when he or she has attached negative associations to their trading. This can come from a long drawdown or after any major loss. A trader will find it difficult to take action when equating action with anticipated negative feelings. A counterbalance of pleasurable feelings must be associated with trading.

To overcome negative associations, focus every day on the best possible outcome for each step of your trading rules until you feel you are in an emotionally positive state. Setting up a habit of good feelings followed by taking the right action is a highly effective way to create positive anchors.

Here is a step-by-step strategy:

1. Remember in detail a positive emotional experience in which you were performing exceptionally well.
2. At the height of the feeling this visualization creates, clasp your hands together and say a meaningful word. An example: "Yes!"
3. Repeat many times until it becomes a strong anchor.
4. Whenever you want to be in a good performance state, clasp your hands and say your trigger word.

Problem 5. The Procrastinating Trader

The trader who finds it hard to take action puts off taking action by giving excuses. Trading is like fighting a war in which your enemies are your own psychological demons. These demons are your darkest secrets, your most extreme emotions and your greatest vulnerabilities. Each time you have to face one of these demons, you fight yourself and your ability to maintain momentum. Without the qualities of tenacity, persistence, and courage, you cannot wage these battles. The part of you that will be victorious is the emotionally vulnerable side.

One way to stay on track is to associate with highly motivated people through books and tapes, in person and at seminars. Have a weekly and daily plan with specific tasks to complete within a given amount of time and play "beat the clock."

Trap 3: Conflict

The third set of traps results from conflicts that are going on within a trader's mind. In order to have a conflict, there must be two opposing sides. One of the major reasons traders find it difficult to make choices is because one part of them wants to follow good trading rules and another part of them has a different agenda. A typical conflict is the trader's fear of losing on one side, and the desire to make profits on the other side. The part of the trader's mind that is more emotionally charged will always gain ascendance, and that is usually the self-destructive side. Consciously, the trader may be telling him- or herself that he or she wants to be successful, disciplined, and happy, but unconsciously may be telling himself (or herself) that success brings pain, that discipline does not guarantee happiness, and that he or she does not deserve to experience joy in his or her life. These negatively charged parts will usually prevail. If these conflicts remain unidentified and unresolved, they will sabotage your best performance and the achievement of your goals.

Some problems that affect traders who are in conflict include:

Problem 1. Conflicting Trading Signals

When a trader's system tells that trader to do one thing, but for some other reason he or she feels it should be a different choice, this conflict will result in late entries, no entries, or choices that don't follow his or her system. Even the finest systems will produce losses, but when following a good system consistently, it will produce more winnings than losses over time. However, a trader who is in conflict because he or she has conflicting goals, intentions, feelings, etc., will not be able to follow his or her system. Here is a neuro-linguistic programming strategy for handling conflicts:

1. Identify a conflict and name the two conflicting parts. See these conflicting parts in your mind's eye. An example: A *trader part* and a *fear part.*
2. Ask yourself to identify the positive intention of each part (all parts of you have a positive intention). An example: The *trader part* wants success and the *fear part* wants to protect you.
3. With the positive intentions in mind, ask the *creative part* of you to come up with three ways these two parts can work together. An example: You will only trade your system after it is fully tested; you will only risk what you can afford to lose, and you will give yourself a reward when you follow your rules for a week.

4. Ask yourself if there are any other parts of you that are in conflict with these two parts working with these new agreements. If there is another part of you that is in conflict with this agreement, start the exercise all over again with the integrated parts and the new part in conflict. When parts of you are in agreement, feel the integration of them in your body.

Problem 2. The Disappointed Parents/Spouse

When a trader's parents or spouse want him or her to be in another profession, the trader can often hear their voice in his (or her) head when he (or she) gets a signal. For example, a trader's logical side tells you to take a good setup, but your emotional side hears "you're risking the education of your children, are you sure you know what you are doing?" He or she feels afraid and guilty. The emotional side wins.

Problem 3. Unconscious Need for Losses

Traders who were "robbed" of something important to them early on in their lives can have sustained feelings of violation. Later on they often fear that if they accumulate wealth, someone or something (like the markets) may take it away. As a result, although traders may tell themselves consciously that they want to be successful, they will create losses themselves. This prevents anyone or anything from violating them again.

Problem 4. Stuck on a Career Plateau

When a trader wants to succeed on a conscious level but is uncomfortable at an unconscious level, higher levels of success become impossible. A common example of this is a trader who feels guilty that a parent (e.g., the father) worked so hard to produce an income when it is so easy for him or her to far exceed the same income. The result of this guilt is conflict producing a self-imposed earnings-ceiling.

Problem 5. Communication Blocking

When traders do not say what they mean and mean what they say to significant people in their lives, it leaves an incompleteness that is disturbing to their nervous system. This unrest intensifies everyday negative emotions. The result is conflict in thought and therefore trading.

Trap 4: Inappropriate Emotional States

The fourth set of traps has to do with being inappropriate with your emotions. Appropriate emotional states for trading are emotional states which produce positive results.

Following are some problems experienced by traders who are in the throes of inappropriate emotional states:

Problem 1. The Frightened Trader

Fear is the number one psychological reason a trader fails. Some of the major fears traders have are:

- *Fear of failure:* When you associate failure with physical and emotional pain and try to avoid these feelings, they will surface during emotionally weak moments.
- *Fear of success:* This fear is developed as a result of not feeling worthy, being afraid of responsibility, or being afraid of the negative beliefs you have about people who are wealthy.
- *Fear of losing money:* You perceive losing money as losing power and/or security. Facing the ridicule of others and the discomfort of the guilt that can follow from having a loss is another reason why traders feel this fear.
- *Fear of being wrong:* This fear emerges when you are trying to avoid the pain and punishment you cause yourself when a trade goes against you.
- *Fear of not being able to continue trading:* You become afraid when you feel threatened that you might have to get the kind of "real job" you don't like. This fear is enhanced

by the realization that you will also lose the tremendous investment of time, energy, and money that you have invested in your trading career.

Here are strategies for handling fear, as well as all of the other inappropriate emotions that stand in the way of good trading:

- Emotional mental rehearsal of contingencies: Consider all of the appropriate emotions for each part of your trading. In other words, what is the appropriate emotional state for you to stalk a trade, enter a trade, be in a trade, and take profit or loss?

  An example of a contingency mental rehearsal would be to visualize all of the possible scenarios for entering a trade. In your mind's eye, see yourself taking the trade in an appropriate emotional state such as: calmness, confidence, attentiveness, focus, and alertness.
- Outlets for emotional release

  1. While doing aerobic exercise, think of the situations in the day that were particularly stressful, and then think of the blessings in your life. The additional oxygen to your system will help dissipate the negative feelings of the day, and the positive thoughts will put you back in a good emotional frame of mind.
  2. Read books, see movies, listen to tapes that trigger intense emotional states. Then, allow yourself to fully experience and be with the feeling until it is complete.

Problem 2. The Greedy Trader

Greed is the second major feeling that will sabotage trading efforts. When a trader lacks a sense of competence and confidence, he or she is vulnerable to addictive behavior. Traders who feel an overwhelming sense of power after a series of windfall trades are highly susceptible to this psychological trap. This emotional state holds them captive in feeling invincible resulting in a violation of all of the rules of their system.

Problem 3. The Trader with Tirades

Traders who display fits of rage to their family and friends after having taken a series of losses destroy a supportive environment. These traders usually blame their problems on something other than themselves like the markets or their broker. Often what follows is additional losses when they try to get even by taking too much risk. Emotional outbursts are a result of stored up emotions and stress.

Problem 4. The Guilty Trader

Guilty feelings from events of the past will make a trader feel undeserving and will cause traders to sabotage their success. These feelings are most prevalent in people whose values and beliefs are molded by traditions which use guilt to control them.

Problem 5. The Worried Trader

Anxiety arises as a result of the anticipation of failure in the future, which comes from remembering failures in the past and then projecting them onto imagined scenarios of losses for the future. Chronic worry depletes a trader's emotional and physical reserves, dulls his or her focus and concentration and can create panic attacks.

Problem 6. The Sorrowful Trader

Sorrow results from perceived losses and over time acts as a curtain between a trader and his or her ability to see what is actually happening in his or her trading. In addition, it can lead to depression, with all of its physical, emotional, and social problems.

Trap 5: Losses and Wins

The fifth set of traps traders can fall into is how they deal with wins and losses. One would imagine that traders would feel uncomfortable taking losses but comfortable with taking profits, since that should be their goal in trading. But, for some, taking profits is not a comfortable experience any more than taking losses is.

Some problems typical of traders who find it difficult to handle losses and wins follow:

Problem 1. The "Loss-Fearing" Trader

When traders first enter into the trading business, they very often are not prepared and therefore suffer many losses. If they learn their lesson and then prepare themselves for good trading, they will still be carrying with them the negative anchors of the losses of when they first started. As a result of these negative anchors, they find it difficult to enter a trade. These losses are remembered as intensely painful experiences to be avoided.

Recognize that most negative events of the past are associated with a loss. When you lose something or someone it creates physical and emotional pain. The more unresolved losses you have, the more likely you will create more losses.

One way to handle the issue of losses is to look for the serendipity in every loss. For example: you can recognize the lesson that needs to be learned from a loss when you go against your rules, or see it as leading to a better opportunity. On the other hand, the most powerful way to handle loss is to use visualization. These same techniques can be applied to problems with handling wins, as well:

1. Visualize yourself making profits and enjoying the process.
2. If you are afraid of the additional responsibility, visualize keeping your responsibility the same while having additional income.
3. If you are uncomfortable about becoming wealthy because you have negative beliefs about money or people with money, give away a percentage of the profits. I recommend that you should see the results of this tithing. Examples: Little League uniforms, a new church organ, a family member needing money for education, and so forth.

Problem 2. The "Suppose I Can't" Trader

When traders begin to earn more money, they often take on more financial responsibilities such as a high mortgage payment and a high lease payment on a new car. These traders give back profits because they are afraid of the additional responsibility they will take on by earning a higher income base.

Problem 3. The Happy Loser

Traders can actually feel relieved in taking losses after a series of winning trades, because the stress they feel when they are winning is too uncomfortable to bear. There are a number of reasons a trader may feel relieved to lose. He may doubt his ability to sustain a winning streak; he may feel unworthy of winning; or he may be certain that his own trading story is all about losses and, expecting them to come at any moment, he is relieved when they finally arrive.

Problem 4. The Uncomfortable Winner

If increased earnings coincided with a serious and painful loss, a profitable run can be uncomfortable from the time of that loss. A trader who is operating under this association will sabotage a winning streak to stop the painful connection of the past loss.

Trap 6: Perceptions

The sixth area of traps has to do with how you create your own reality. Misperceptions or negative perceptions create missed opportunities. We take in information through our senses which then creates our attitudes, beliefs, and values. These perceptions will be the deciding factor in our actions and therefore our level of success.

Some perceptual traps into which traders fall include:

Problem 1. The Undeserving Trader

Many traders do not believe they deserve to be successful and earn a lot of money. In order to make money in trading it must be one of your top values. Values are your strongest held beliefs and therefore motivate you to compelling actions. If your top value in being a trader is peace of mind, then continues down in importance with freedom and other values follow, but money is not among the top five values, your actions are less likely to create wealth in your trading. (To change a value requires the assistance of a professional therapist or coach.)

Problem 2. The Hardworking Trader

Many traders think that the harder they work the more money they will earn. This equation is usually one they learned at home or in their schooling and can become a deeply held belief. If you work hard and not smart, you will eventually burn yourself out of good performance. Traders need to learn that part of becoming a successful trader is learning how to balance their personal lives with their professional lives so that they have the energy and motivation for the long run. If you view your rewards in life as limited by the amount of effort you expend, this attitude will determine how you will experience life and your trading.

Problem 3. The Unworthy Profession

Many traders secretly believe that trading does not give any value to society. It is difficult to give trading your best efforts when you believe that what you do has no real value and may even be unworthy or parasitic in nature.

Here is a neuro-linguistic programming strategy for changing your attitudes and beliefs:

1. Which attitude or belief does not serve to benefit you in a positive direction? (Such as, making money means more responsibility.)
2. If you were to continue to have this belief, what direction do you think your trading would take in the next five years? (Be sure to paint a bleak picture adding a lot of detail to stir negative emotions.)
3. What type of beliefs could you have that would take you in the direction you want to go? (Examples would be: (1)

with more money I have more options, one of which is to not take on more responsibility. (2) My life would be a lot more interesting with more responsibility.)

4. Now see yourself in five years with these kinds of beliefs. (The beliefs you choose should stir you into very positive thinking or choose other beliefs.)

5. Ask yourself how you feel about the old belief. If you add enough positive pictures it should no longer be an option to keep the old belief.

Trap 7: Negative Behaviors

The seventh area of traps has to do with the choices you make and the actions you take. One choice of action in trading can make the difference between a winning or losing year.

Traps that traders experience when they engage in negative behavior follow.

Problem 1. The Unbalanced Life

When all of the areas of your life are not satisfied, any one of them can sabotage your efforts in trading in order to get your attention. This signal given by your body is meant to get your attention so you will do something about it. Most traders don't recognize these signals as being important enough to make changes.

The first step in balancing yourself is to time-manage the activities important in your life with the significant people in your life. Make a plan which includes setting a time when you will be able to do the things you cannot get done now in the future. Try to make the significant people in your life as comfortable with your program as possible, otherwise they may create ways to undermine your efforts.

Problem 2. The Addicted Trader

Addictive substances exhaust the adrenal glands, which will affect the amount of focus and energy you have, and therefore the choices of actions you take. To overcome addictions, whether they are physical, emotional, or mental, usually requires professional help.

Problem 3. The Untrustworthy Trader

When you do not keep your agreements you set up a pattern with your neurology (nervous system or mind) that it is okay not to follow your trading rules. All behavior patterns feel comfortable and natural even if they are not in our best interest. If you are not used to a pattern of following through on what you say you will do, you will not get the support of your neurology to follow the rules of your system.

One strategy for creating trust between you and yourself is to write down specific agreements or goals and simple tasks which you know you can complete. Attach a reward to their completion. Make sure you put a check after each task completed. This will act as an anchor for a new pattern and give you a feeling of accomplishment. Increase the tasks as you become better at keeping agreements.

Problem 4. The Critical Trader

The habit of critical self-talk leads to conflicts and mistrust of your ability. Mistrust always leads to conflict, which leads to indecision or no decision.

A successful strategy in overcoming critical exchanges is to become a translator for your internal and external conversations by translating the critical voice into a complementary voice whenever you hear yourself or others criticize.

Problem 5. The Unhealthy Trader

The trader who eats badly, fails to exercise, puts too much time into work, and does not get enough rest and relaxation is not able to summon the energy and vitality that is required for successful trading performance. Energy keeps your focus clear and helps to stabilize your emotions. When your energy is low, you are more likely to continue to make bad health choices and bad trading choices as well.

Examples of good health choices (always consult a physician before taking on a new health regime) follow:

1. Food
- Lean meats and other proteins
- Fresh fruits and vegetables and juices
- Minimum of pastas and grains
- Minimum of unsaturated fat, such as olive oil
- Lots of purified water
- Best cooking is boiled or steamed (all other choices compromise your health to a greater or lesser degree)

2. Relaxation
- A minimum of six hours of restful sleep, preferably before 11:00 P.M.
- A minimum of one hour of relaxation before sleep
- Learn meditation from a professional teacher

3. Exercise
- A minimum of 20 minutes of aerobic exercise that makes you sweat

Problem 6. The Undisciplined Trader

Discipline is the number one key ingredient to becoming a successful trader and the lack of it their downfall. If you cannot follow your own rules you are not disciplined. The three key ingredients in being disciplined are motivation, a plan of action, and believing that you can (refer to strategies section in this chapter dealing with these issues).

Problem 7. The Disorganized Trader

Highly successful traders are organized individuals because good trading demands it. Gaining control over the chaos in your life should be started one small step at a time because attempts to bring order to chaos all at once are usually too overwhelming. Keeping things organized is less time consuming in the long run than being disorganized and will reduce the stress that comes with constantly looking for things. You have to make a habit of and be willing to have a place for everything and keep everything in its place and, also, be willing to let go of those things that are cluttering up your environment. You should consider delegating or hiring someone to take on some of the responsibility of your organization. Always consider the value of your time and energy, and you will probably find it is a good choice.

Problem 8. The Unrewarded Trader

If a trader does not feel reward in trading or from the trading results, he or she will not find a reason to trade at a top level of performance. Problems occur for traders who don't reward themselves. All of us are programmed from childhood to expect rewards for good action. Positive emotions follow when you receive these rewards. Our neurology would rather support us in feeling positive because health and well-being are a natural state of mind. It is important to find appropriate rewards that will stimulate you into positive action so that positive trading results will follow.

A successful strategy for learning to reward yourself is to make a continuous wish list of all the things you want to have for the rest of your life. Attach one of these items from your wish list to each new level of success. Once you have achieved that next level of success, be sure to give yourself the reward that was attached to that achievement.

Problem 9. The Control-Freak Trader

When you try to control anything, it is a sure signal that you are out of control. Negative thinking leads to out-of-control trading. In order to overcome the need to control the markets or other people, you must overcome these insecurities in yourself and your trading decisions. You will feel insecure about your trading until you believe your system will give you positive returns. Testing will help you build trust and therefore overcome your insecurities.

Problem 10. The Perfect Trader

Perfectionist thinking causes most people to create unnecessary tensions and adds excessive tasks to everything you try to accomplish. Traders who were raised in a family where whatever they did was not good enough might find they can never complete a system. These traders will also feel that no setup is good enough to risk money.

Reframe the idea of perfection by setting a goal of aiming for the best possible outcome within a specific time frame. This new way of thinking will give you better results without the stress.

Trap 8: Environmental Issues

The eighth area of traps you will find in your environment, both physical and social, and how it affects your performance as a trader.

Following are some traps which traders fall into because of the influence of negative environmental issues on their trading:

Problem 1. Life Changes for the Trader

Traders who have just experienced a major change in their lives (new marriage, new baby, new job, new house, etc.) are more likely than not to find that their trading is out of kilter for a considerable period while they adjust to the change. Even positive changes can wreak havoc with a trader's performance. When you are going through major changes either stop trading or lighten up on your trading activity.

Problem 2. The Trader Under Attack

Traders will create anxiety to perform when the significant people in their lives believe trading is gambling and want them to get a "real job" to guarantee security.

In order to neutralize negative exchanges that take place at home (or elsewhere), first notice these common patterns of conversations with the people in your life. Exchange the negative patterns with positive responses. For example, in response to this angry confrontation from your spouse, "You're late as usual for dinner, and everything is getting cold," your reply could be, "You're right and I'm so sorry. Fortunately, your food tastes good even when it's cold. And I'm so lucky to have you in my life." It is okay to ask for emotional support. Let the important people in your life know that it would be to their advantage to give you emotional support. For example: "I would love to be able to give you what you want. This is more likely to happen if our conversations are more positive, and I intend to do whatever I can to make it so."

Problem 3. The Stressed-Out Trader

If a trader gets no relief from stress because of being obsessed with trading and does not have any other real life beyond trading, he or she will ultimately create losses. One of the chief causes of stress for a trader is being undercapitalized. If undercapitalization is a problem, do not trade until you have enough money to trade your system. Fear anchors will develop the minute you have a period of drawdown that can force you out of trading permanently. If possible, work for an institution or someone who will invest in you as a trader.

Problem 4. The Polluted Trader

Spending long hours in a room that is polluted by cigarette smoke, chemical smells and emissions, too much electric current, mold, or substances to which the trader is allergic, can have a long-term impact on a trader's career. A working environment that is too noisy, quiet, dark, cold, hot, crowded, depressing, uncomfortable, or chaotic will create stress and sap a trader's energy and focus. You have thus created a physical environment that is not conducive to your best trading performance.

It is important to clean up your environment if it is polluted. This means that you must remove as many pollutants as possible. Get an air purifier if necessary. Use a screen protector on your monitor. Take breaks away from your environment into nature when possible.

Summary

A trader needs a strong psychological foundation to stay disciplined and to be able to follow his or her methodology so that he or she will consistently make a profit.

In turn, the strong psychological foundation needed for trading success rests firmly on a balanced life. To achieve this balanced life, a trader has to make a commitment to attending to all of the needs in his or her life, including his or her emotional and spiritual well-being, social needs and relationship, health and education, as well as career and financial security. If a trader neglects any one of these areas, his or her foundation could be thrown off balance and his or her trading career will be affected. Left unattended, the results can be a series of losses as well as problems in his or her personal life that can also put an end to trading.

Attention to the psychological issues in your life will put you ahead of the game and prevent many unnecessary losses. And if you continue to develop your resources, you will be ready for each new level of success in your trading as well as the rest of your life.

APPENDIX A

COMPONENTS OF THE DOW

JONES INDUSTRIAL AVERAGE

ALD	Allied-Signal Inc	HWP	Hewlett Packard
AA	Alcoa Aluminum	IBM	International Business Machines
AXP	American Express	IP	International Paper
T	AT&T	JNJ	Johnson & Johnson
BA	Boeing	MCD	McDonalds
CAT	Caterpillar	MRK	Merck
CHV	Chevron	MMM	Minnesota Mining & Manufacturing
KO	Coca Cola	JPM	Morgan JP
DIS	Disney	MO	Philip Morris
DD	Dupont	PG	Procter & Gamble
EK	Eastman Kodak	S	Sears
XON	Exxon	TRV	Travelers Group Inc
GE	General Electric	UK	Union Carbide
GM	General Motors	UTX	United Technologies
GT	Goodyear	WMT	Wal-Mart Stores Inc.

Note: this table was changed just prior to publication of this book, as the components of the DJIA were modified March 17, 1997. Four stocks were removed from the original (Bethlehem Steel, Texaco, Woolworth, Westinghouse) and four stocks were added (Travelers Group Inc, WalMart, Hewlett-Packard, and Johnson & Johnson). The divisor was modified to keep the index stable from the close of 3/16/97 to the open of 3/17/97.

APPENDIX B
EXCHANGES

Chicago Mercantile Exchange (CME)

	Symbol	Delivery Months	Trading Hours (ET)
AUSTRALIAN DOLLAR	AD	H, M, U, Z (cash = A)	08:20 AM–03:00 PM
BRITISH POUND	BP	H, M, U, Z (cash = A)	08:20 AM–03:00 PM
BRITISH POUND, rolling spot	RP	H, M, U, Z (X = daily adj)	08:00 AM–03:00 PM
CANADIAN DOLLAR	CD	H, M, U, Z (cash = A)	08:20 AM–03:00 PM
CATTLE, Feeder	FC	F, H, J, K, Q, U, V, X	10:05 AM–02:00 PM
CATTLE, Live	LC	G, J, M, Q, V, Z	10:05 AM–02:00 PM
D-MARK/YEN (settled in yen)	DJ	H, M, U, Z	08:20 AM–03:00 PM
DEUTSCHE MARK	DM	H, M, U, Z (cash = A)	08:20 AM–03:00 PM
DEUTSCHE MARK, rolling spot	RD	H, M, U, Z (X = daily adj)	08:00 AM–03:00 PM
EURODOLLAR	ED	H, M, U, Z	08:20 AM–03:00 PM
EUROMARK	EK	H, M, U, Z	08:20 AM–03:00 PM
FRENCH FRANC	FR	H, M, U, Z (cash = A)	08:20 AM–03:00 PM
FT-SE 100 INDEX (London)	FI	H, M, U, Z (cash = FN XO)	09:30 AM–04:30 PM

Chicago Mercantile Exchange (CME) *(Continued)*

	Symbol	Delivery Months	Trading Hours (ET)
GOLDMAN-SACHS INDEX	GI	G, J, M, Q, V, Z	09:15 AM– 03:15 PM
GOLDMAN-SACHS INDEX, Cash	GN	X	08:20 AM– 05:05 PM
HOGS, Live	LH	G, J, M, N, Q, V, Z	10:10 AM– 02:00 PM
LIBOR (LONDON INTER-BANK RATE)	EM	ALL MONTHS	08:00 AM– 03:00 PM
LUMBER, Random Length	LB	F, H, K, N, U, X	10:00 AM– 02:05 PM
MAJOR MARKET INDEX	MM	ALL MONTHS (cash = X)	09:15 AM– 04:15 PM
MEXICAN PESO	ME	H, M, U, Z (cash = A)	08:20 AM– 03:00 PM
NIKKEI 225 STOCK INDEX (Japan)	NK	H, M, U, Z	09:00 AM– 04:15 PM
JAPANESE YEN	JY	H, M, U, Z (cash = A)	08:20 AM– 03:00 PM
JAPANESE YEN, rolling spot	RY	H, M, U, Z (X = daily adj.)	08:20 AM– 03:00 PM
JAPANESE YEN, currency forward	FE	ALL MONTHS	08:20 AM– 03:00 PM
PORK BELLIES	PB	G, H, K, N, Q	10:10 AM– 02:00 PM
RUSSELL 2000 INDEX	RL	H, M, U, Z (cash = IU XO)	09:30 AM– 04:15 PM
S&P 400 MIDCAP INDEX	MD	H, M, U, Z (cash = ID XO)	09:30 AM– 04:15 PM
S&P 500 INDEX	SP	H, M, U, Z (cash = IN XO)	09:30 AM– 04:15 PM
SWISS FRANC	SF	H, M, U, Z (cash = A)	08:20 AM– 03:00 PM
T-BILLS (90 DAY)	TB	H, M, U, Z	08:20 AM– 03:00 PM
T-BILLS (1 YEAR)	YR	H, M, U, Z	08:20 AM– 03:00 PM

Commodity Exchange (COMX)

	Symbol	Delivery Months	Trading Hours (ET)
HIGH GRADE COPPER	HG	ALL MONTHS	08:10 AM–02:00 PM
EUROTOP 100 INDEX (Europe)	ER	H, M, U, Z (cash = A)	07:30 AM–04:15 PM
GOLD	GC	G, J, M, Q, V, Z	08:20 AM–02:30 PM
SILVER	SI	H, K, N, U, Z	08:25 AM–02:25 PM

Coffee, Sugar, and Cocoa (CSC)

	Symbol	Delivery Months	Trading Hours (ET)
BRAZILIAN-DIFFERENTIAL COFFEE	KB	H, K, N, U, Z	09:05 AM–01:58 PM
CHEDDAR CHEESE	EZ	G, K, N, U, X	02:15 PM–03:15 PM
COCOA (Metric)	CC	H, K, N, U, Z	09:00 AM–02:00 PM
COFFEE "C"	KC	H, K, N, U, Z	09:15 AM–02:05 PM
NONFAT DRY MILK	MU	G, K, N, U, X	02:15 PM–03:15 PM
SUGAR #11	SB	H, K, N, V	09:30 AM–01:20 PM
SUGAR #14	SE	F, H, K, N, U, V	09:10 AM–01:15 PM
WHITE SUGAR	WS	F, H, K, N	09:15 AM–01:20 PM

New York Cotton Exchange (CEC)

	Symbol	Delivery Months	Trading Hours (ET)
BRITISH POUND	YP	H, M, U, Z	08:05 AM–03:00 PM
B-POUND/D-MARK CROSS RATE	MP	H, M, U, Z	09:05 AM–03:00 PM

New York Cotton Exchange (CEC) (Continued)

	Symbol	Delivery Months	Trading Hours (ET)
COTTON #2	CT	H, K, N, V, Z	10:30 AM–02:40 PM
COTTON (Cotlock)	CI	H, K, N, V, Z	10:30 AM–02:40 PM
DEUTSCH MARK	YM	H, M, U, Z	08:05 AM–03:00 PM
D-MARK/F-FRANC CROSS RATE	MF	H, M, U, Z	09:05 AM–03:00 PM
D-MARK/LIRA CROSS RATE	ML	H, M, U, Z	09:05 AM–03:00 PM
D-MARK/YEN CROSS RATE	MY	H, M, U, Z	09:05 AM–03:00 PM
JAPANESE YEN	YY	H, M, U, Z	08:05 AM–03:00 PM
ORANGE JUICE (Frozen Concentrated)	JO	F, H, K, N, U, X	10:15 AM–02:15 PM
SWISS FRANC	YF	H, M, U, Z	08:05 AM–03:00 PM
T-NOTE (2 year)	TW	ALL MONTHS	08:20 AM–03:00 PM
T-NOTE (5 Year)	FY	ALL MONTHS	08:20 AM–03:00 PM
US DOLLAR INDEX	DX	H, M, U, Z	03:00 AM–03:00 PM
		(cash = A – 24 hrs)	

New York Futures Exchange (CEC)

	Symbol	Delivery Months	Trading Hours (ET)
CRB INDEX	CR	H, K, N, U, Z	09:40 AM–02:45 PM
CRB INDEX, Cash	CR	A	08:15 AM–04:30 PM
NYSE COMPOSITE INDEX	YX	H, M, U, Z (cash = A)	09:30 AM–04:15 PM
NYSE UTILITIES INDEX	YU	H, M, U, Z (cash = A)	09:30 AM–04:15 PM

New York Mercantile Exchange (NYME)

	Symbol	Delivery Months	Trading Hours (ET)
CRUDE OIL (Light)	CL	ALL MONTHS	09:45 AM–03:10 PM
CRUDE OIL (Sour)	SC	ALL MONTHS	09:35 AM–03:20 PM
GASOLINE, UNLEADED	HU	ALL MONTHS	09:50 AM–03:10 PM
GASOLINE, UNLEADED (Gulf Coast)	GU	ALL MONTHS	09:40 AM–03:10 PM
GASOLINE, UNL/CRUDE OIL SPREAD	UC	ALL MONTHS (cash = A)	09:50 AM–03:10 PM
HEATING OIL/CRUDE OIL SPREAD	HC	ALL MONTHS (cash = A)	09:50 AM–03:10 PM
HEATING OIL	HO	ALL MONTHS	09:50 AM–03:10 PM
NATURAL GAS	NG	ALL MONTHS	10:00 AM–03:10 PM
PALLADIUM**	PA	H, M, U, Z	08:10 AM–02:20 PM
PLATINUM**&++	PL	F, J, N, V	08:20 AM–02:30 PM
PROPANE++	PN	ALL MONTHS	09:55 AM–03:00 PM

Kansas City Board of Trade (KCBT)

	Symbol	Delivery Months	Trading Hours (ET)
VALUE LINE INDEX	KV	H, M, U, Z	09:30 AM–04:15 PM
VALUE LINE INDEX, Cash (Geometric)	XV	L	09:30 AM–04:00 PM
VALUE LINE INDEX, Cash (Arithmetic)	VA	A	09:30 AM–04:00 PM
VALUE LINE INDEX, MINI	MV	H, M, U, Z	09:30 AM–04:15 PM
WESTERN NATURAL GAS	KC	ALL MONTHS	09:30 AM–03:30 PM
WHEAT	KW	H, K, N, U, Z	10:30 AM–02:15 PM

Minneapolis Grain Exchange (MGE)

	Symbol	Delivery Months	Trading Hours (ET)
OATS	OM	H, K, N, U, Z	10:30 AM–02:30 PM
WHEAT, Hard Red	MW	H, K, N, U, Z	10:30 AM–02:15 PM
WHEAT, White	NW	H, K, N, U, Z	10:30 AM–02:15 PM
WHITE SHRIMP	SH	H, M, U, Z	10:40 AM–02:30 PM

Midamerica Exchange (MIDA)

	Symbol	Delivery Months	Trading Hours (ET)
BRITISH POUNDS	XP	H, M, U, Z	08:20 AM–03:15 PM
CANADIAN DOLLARS	XD	H, M, U, Z	08:20 AM–03:15 PM
CATTLE, Live	XL	G, J, , Q, V, Z	09:45 AM–02:15 PM
CORN	XC	H, K, N, U, Z	10:30 AM–02:45 PM
DEUTSCHE MARKS	XM	H, M, U, Z	08:20 AM–03:15 PM
EURODOLLARS	UD	H, M, U, Z	08:20 AM–04:15 PM
GOLD	XK	ALL MONTHS	08:20 AM–02:40 PM
HOGS, Live	XH	G, J, M, N, Q, V, Z	09:45 AM–02:15 PM
JAPANESE YEN	XJ	H, M, U, Z	08:20 AM–03:15 PM
OATS	XO	H, K, N, U, Z	10:30 AM–02:45 PM
PLATINUM	XU	F, J, N, V + nearest 3 months	08:20 AM–02:40 PM
SILVER	XY	ALL MONTHS	08:25 AM–02:40 PM
SOYBEANS	XS	F, H, K, N, Q, U, X	10:30 AM–02:45 PM
SOYBEAN MEAL	XE	F, H, K, N, Q, U, V, Z	10:30 AM–02:45 PM

Midamerica Exchange (MIDA) *(Continued)*

	Symbol	Delivery Months	Trading Hours (ET)
SOYBEAN OIL	XR	F, H, K, N, Q, U, V, Z	10:30 AM–02:45 PM
SWISS FRANCS	XF	H, M, U, Z	08:20 AM–03:15 PM
T-BILLS	XT	H, M, U, Z	08:20 AM–03:15 PM
T-BONDS	XB	H, M, U, Z	08:20 AM–04:15 PM
T-NOTES (5 year)	XV	H, M, U, Z	08:20 AM–04:15 PM
T-NOTES (10 year)	XN	H, M, U, Z	08:20 AM–04:15 PM
WHEAT	XW	H, K, N, U, Z	10:30 AM–02:45 PM

APPENDIX C

ANNUAL CLOSING VALUES OF THE DOW JONES INDUSTRIAL AVERAGE AND YEAR OVER YEAR INCREASE

Year	Close	Return
1951	266	
1952	286	7%
1953	281	−2%
1954	394	40%
1955	485	23%
1956	492	2%
1957	437	−11%
1958	566	30%
1959	671	19%
1960	610	−9%
1961	728	20%
1962	648	−11%
1963	760	17%
1964	867	14%
1965	955	10%
1966	801	−16%
1967	887	11%
1968	968	9%
1969	789	−19%
1970	822	4%
1971	870	6%
1972	1,020	17%
1973	824	−19%
1974	597	−28%

Year	Close	Return
1975	841	41%
1976	977	16%
1977	819	−16%
1978	808	−1%
1979	836	3%
1980	946	13%
1981	878	−7%
1982	1,033	18%
1983	1,258	22%
1984	1,189	−5%
1985	1,517	28%
1986	1,924	27%
1987	1,911	−1%
1988	2,149	12%
1989	2,728	27%
1990	2,633	−3%
1991	3,169	20%
1992	3,301	4%
1993	3,754	14%
1994	3,834	2%
1995	5,117	33%
1996	6,813	33%
AVERAGE RETURN		9%

APPENDIX D

MARGIN REQUIREMENTS AS OF FEBRUARY 1, 1997— ARRANGED ALPHABETICALLY BY COMMODITY

Commodity	Initial	Maintenance	Spreads
10-Year Note	$1,755	$1,300	350
2-Year Note	$1,080	$800	350
5-Year Note	$1,215	$900	350
Australian Dollar	$1,317	$975	200
BC (Maxi)	$9,450	$7,000	750
Bean Oil	$540	$400	200
British Pound	$1,890	$1,400	200
Canadian Dollar	$507	$375	200
Cocoa	$560	$400	250
Coffee	$2,800	$2,000	750
Copper	$2,160	$1,600	600
Corn	$405	$300	200
Cotton	$1,330	$1,000	600
CRB Index	$2,000	$1,750	750
Crude Oil	$2,970	$2,200	540
Deutsche Mark	$1,215	$900	200
Dollar Index	$1,065	$800	400
Eurodollar	$540	$400	300
Euro-Top (CMX)	$3,000	$3,000	1000
Feeder Cattle	$945	$700	200
Gold (CMX)	$1,013	$750	450
Gold (Kilo)	$203	$150	100
Heating Oil	$2,700	$2,000	540
Japanese Yen	$1,485	$1,100	400

Commodity	Initial	Maintenance	Spreads
Kansas City Wheat	$1,000	$1,000	400
Live Cattle	$608	$450	300
Live Hogs	$878	$650	275
Lumber	$1,875	$1,250	600
Mid-Cap 400	$3,713	$2,750	750
Mini Value Line	$1,500	$1,200	500
Municipal Bonds	$2,295	$1,700	350
NASDAQ 100	$3,510	$2,600	500
Natural Gas	$8,505	$6,300	3400
Nikkel Index	$4,725	$3,500	750
NYSE Composite Index	$3,500	$3,000	750
Oats	$540	$400	200
Orange Juice	$1,330	$1,000	375
Palladium	$810	$600	400
Peso	$2,500	$2,000	500
Platinum	$1,215	$900	400
Pork Bellies	$1,485	$1,100	
Rough Rice	$675	$500	250
S&P 500 Index	$15,120	$13,500	1000
Silver—1000 Ounce	$270	$200	100
Silver—5000 Ounce	$1,890	$1,400	500
Soy Meal	$810	$600	400
Soybeans	$1,350	$1,000	500
Sugar	$580	$400	250
Swiss Frank	$1,688	$1,250	200
T-Peter	$675	$500	237
Unleaded Gas	$2,700	$2,000	675
US Treasury Bonds	$2,700	$2,000	350
Value Line	$7,500	$6,000	750
Wheat (CBOT)	$945	$700	350

APPENDIX E

MARGIN REQUIREMENTS AS OF FEBRUARY 1, 1997— ARRANGED IN ASCENDING ORDER BY INITIAL MARGIN

Commodity	Initial	Maintenance	Spreads
Gold (Kilo)	$203	$150	100
Silver—1000 Ounce	$270	$200	100
Corn	$405	$300	200
Canadian Dollar	$507	$375	200
Bean Oil	$540	$400	200
Eurodollar	$540	$400	300
Oats	$540	$400	200
Cocoa	$560	$400	250
Sugar	$560	$400	250
Live Cattle	$608	$450	300
Rough Rice	$675	$500	250
T-Peter	$675	$500	237
Palladium	$810	$600	400
Soy Meal	$810	$600	400
Live Hogs	$878	$650	275
Feeder Cattle	$945	$700	200
Wheat (CBOT)	$945	$700	350
Kansas City Wheat	$1,000	$1,000	400
Gold (CMX)	$1,013	$750	450
Dollar Index	$1,065	$800	400
2-Year Note	$1,080	$800	350
5-Year Note	$1,215	$900	350
Deutsche Mark	$1,215	$900	200
Platinum	$1,215	$900	400

Commodity	Initial	Maintenance	Spreads
Australian Dollar	$1,317	$975	200
Cotton	$1,330	$1,000	600
Orange Juice	$1,330	$1,000	375
Soybeans	$1,350	$1,000	500
Japanese Yen	$1,485	$1,100	400
Pork Bellies	$1,485	$1,100	
Mini Value Line	$1,500	$1,200	500
Swiss Frank	$1,688	$1,250	200
10-Year Note	$1,755	$1,300	350
Lumber	$1,875	$1,250	600
British Pound	$1,890	$1,400	200
Silver—5000 Ounce	$1,890	$1,400	500
CRB Index	$2,000	$1,750	750
Copper	$2,160	$1,600	600
Municipal Bonds	$2,295	$1,700	350
Peso	$2,500	$2,000	500
Heating Oil	$2,700	$2,000	540
Unleaded Gas	$2,700	$2,000	675
US Treasury Bonds	$2,700	$2,000	350
Coffee	$2,800	$2,000	750
Crude Oil	$2,970	$2,200	540
Euro-Top (CMX)	$3,000	$3,000	1000
NYSE Composite Index	$3,500	$3,000	750
NASDAQ 100	$3,510	$2,600	500
Mid-Cap 400	$3,713	$2,750	750
Nikkel Index	$4,725	$3,500	750
Value Line	$7,500	$6,000	750
Natural Gas	$8,505	$6,300	3400
BC (Maxi)	$9,450	$7,000	750
S&P 500 Index	$15,120	$13,500	1000

APPENDIX F
WHO'S WHO IN TRADING

A former psychoanalyst who is highly regarded as a technical analyst, Gerald Appel publishes *Systems and Forecasts* and is the originator of the MACD (Moving Average Convergence-Divergence) trading method. Jerry is a well known contributor to the literature of technical analysis and is an active trader in bonds and stock index futures.

Nauzer J. Balzara is an Associate Professor of Finance at Northeastern Illinois University, Chicago, and an active trader in the futures and options markets. He has a PhD in money and financial markets from Columbia University's Graduate School of Business, New York.

The *Barclay Institutional Report* is published quarterly by Barclay Trading Group, Ltd., 201 N. 2nd St., Ste 304, Fairfield, IA 52556, (515) 472-3456.

John Bollinger, CFA, CMT is best known as the originator of Bollinger Bands. Many investors are familiar with his work from his many years as FNN's Chief Market Analyst and for his market commentary on CNBC. He has published the *Capital Growth Letter* since 1988 and is President of Bollinger Capital Management.

William F. Eng is an international lecturer and workshop instructor on trading techniques and trading psychology. He has raised over $25,000,000 for stock and futures money managers. For over 20 years Eng was a member of the Chicago Board Options Exchange, Chicago Board of Trade, MidAmerica Commodity Exchange, and

Pacific Coast Stock Exchange where he traded for his own accounts. He has written for *Barron's, Futures, Intermarket, Stocks & Commodities,* and the *Wall Street Journal.*

Futures magazine is published monthly by Futures Communications. See your local bookstore or call (800) 972-9316.

Futures Truth is an organization in Hendersonville, NC that keeps track of the performance of over 150 publicly offered trading systems. Founder John Hill can be reached at (704-697-0273).

Kennedy Gammage is editor and publisher of The Richland Report, an investment advisory newsletter based in La Jolla, CA since 1976. Ken holds a Bachelor's degree in Commerce from the University of North Carolina and an MBA from the Harvard Business School. He is familiar to viewers of CNBC, Chicago's WCIU-TV Channel 26, Los Angeles KWHY-TV Channel 22, and as a panelist, lecturer, and commentator nationwide.

Joe Granville has published the *Granville Market Letter* since 1963. In his long career as a stock market analyst, he gained prominence in the financial world in the early '60s when he authored the first of many trend-setting works on technical analysis. Granville quickly attracted national attention in January and September 1981 when he gave a sell signal and the market promptly collapsed. Granville is a pure technician; his OBV theory is a strict following of supply and demand numbers. The *Hulbert Financial Digest* rated the *Granville Market Letter* #1 for 1997 with an overall gain of 89.4%.

International Traders Research, Inc., based in La Jolla, CA, publishes *The Stark Report,* (619) 459-0818.

Managed Account Reports publishes the *Quarterly Performance Report.* For more information contact Lois Peltz at (212) 213-6202.

Ed Seykota is perhaps one of the least known, yet one of the best traders of our time. Ed developed the first commercial computerized trading system.

Ted Tesser is a Certified Public Accountant, licensed by the State of New York, and a member of the New York State Society of Certified Public Accountants. He graduated from Tufts University, Magna Cum Laude, and has a Master's Degree in Accounting from New York University, Graduate School of Business Administration, with a specialty in Investment Related Taxation.

BIBLIOGRAPHY
AND SOURCES

Arnold, Curtis M. *PPS Trading System,* New York: McGraw Hill, 1995.

Babcock, Bruce, Jr. *The Dow Jones-Irwin Guide to Trading Systems,* New York: Dow Jones-Irwin, 1989.

Balsara, Nauzer J. *Money Management Strategies for Futures Traders,* New York: John Wiley & Sons, 1992.

Bernstein, Jake. *Short Term Futures Trading,* MBH, 1992.

Chande, Tushar and Stanley Kroll. *The New Technical Trader,* New York: John Wiley & Sons, 1994.

Colby & Meyers. *The Encyclopedia of Technical Market Indicators,* New York: McGraw Hill, 1988.

Connors, Laurence A., and Linda Bradford Raschke. *Street Smarts,* Malibu, CA: M. Gordon Publishing Co. 1995.

Eng, William. *The Technical Analysis of Stocks, Options & Futures,* Concord, ON: Irwin, 1988.

Krutsinger, Joe. *The Trading Systems ToolKit,* Concord, ON: Irwin, 1994.

Murphy, John J. *Technical Analysis of the Futures Markets,* Upper Saddle River, NJ: Prentice Hall, 1986.

Sweeney, John. *Maximum Adverse Excursion,* New York: John Wiley & Sons, 1997.

Williams, Larry. *The Definitive Guide to Futures Trading,* Brightwaters, NY: Windsor Books, 1988.

INDEX